NOVEMBER SPAWNED A MONSTER

BERNIE SLAVEN
WITH

MARTIN NEAL

Copyright 2015 7 Enterprises Ltd
All rights reserved.
The moral rights of the authors has been asserted.
First published in Great Britain by 7 Enterprises Ltd 2015

ISBN no 978-0-9560684-5-3

Author Bernie Slaven with Martin Neal

Cover design by Graeme Bandeira.

Printed in Singapore by Tien Wah Press.

RRP
£15.99

"Deep down there are likely to be a great many people who agree with you – but for various reasons are reluctant to step forward and declare what they truly believe. The person who courts popularity usually conveys a dishonest message. A person who conveys an honest message is seldom popular."

AUTOGRAPH

To JAMES
HAPPY BIRTHDAY
UP THE BORO!

ACKNOWLEDGEMENTS

I would like to say thanks to Martin Neal who I met up with on a weekly basis for a coffee in the lovely setting at Gisborough hall, he was able to translate all my scribbled notes into this readable book.

Thanks also to Graeme Bandeira for a great cover.
I also have to say thanks to Steve and everyone at Shutter Media Middlesbrough for helping with
photos etc.

Thanks to Seven Enterprises for all the hard word formatting and publishing the book.

FOREWORD

WHEN I first spoke with the newly appointed Century Radio managing director following the Capital Radio takeover back in 2000, he described to me the format he had in mind.

At first I wasn't all that impressed but then I started to warm to what he was describing.

"I see the Legends programme as a two-hour, three-cornered boxing match, with three of you in there each defending your own corner, which is your club of course, then coming out and attacking the other two corners, giving them hell!"

It was a great scenario for radio, especially with the added sparkle of it being a phone-in, callers with you or against you, sides being taken, it could be more competitive than the football we were to discuss.

He then told me I would be joined in the studio by Eric Gates and Bernie Slaven. I knew Eric to a degree, but Bernie? Well all I did know was that if you wrote him a letter and put his address as 'The Six Yard Box' it would find him.

That's where he lived and worked as a player, and very effectively and successfully I must add, but could he cope with the confines of an even smaller space, the radio studio?

Much to my delight Bernie was a studio natural and seemed to know the ultra-strict rule book of radio to the letter enabling him to take a situation just to the limit without ever transgressing.

This lively and vocal lad from humble Glaswegian beginnings seemed to have an etymological knowledge allied to an unfettered imagination that not only made him a joy across the airwaves but an imaginative writer of both articles and books.

I look forward to purchasing a copy of this, his latest tome. Well you don't think he's going to give one to me, do you? I said he's a good friend, but I also said he's from Glasgow and that means I won't even get a discount.

But Bernie, I have to say, I do miss our daily verbal joustings.

Good luck in all you do and also to all your readers.

Malcolm Macdonald

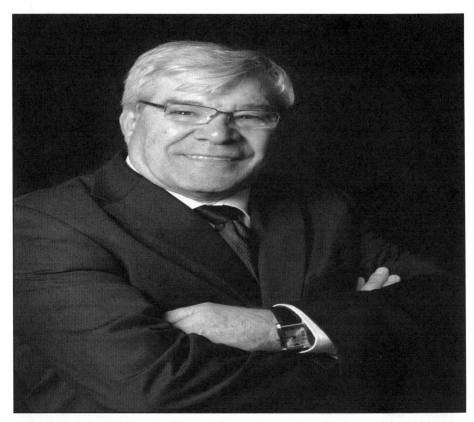

DEDICATION

I would like to dedicate this book, to my late father
Shug.
Without his dedication, love and encouragement I
would not have made it as a professional footballer.

CHAPTERS

30-YEAR ROLLERCOASTER

IF you'd have told me when I was a kid growing up in Glasgow that I was going to come to England and spend more time there than I did in Scotland, I wouldn't have believed you!

But here we are 30 years on and it's been a remarkable journey and I've sampled pretty much everything along the way. I was born on November 13, 1960, and in the words of my favourite musician and songwriter, Morrissey, it seems that month may well have spawned a monster. There have been ups and downs, I've made friends and I've made enemies but when I jumped on a train at Glasgow's Queen Street station on October 2nd 1985 after being invited for a trial at Middlesbrough, my objectives were to enjoy full-time football, play in the top flight, play at Wembley and get international recognition. I'm very proud to have achieved all of that in the past 30 years.

After playing for Morton brief spell at Airdrie then Queen of the

South I made my mark with Albion Rovers but I had confidence I could do it at a higher level and I'm pretty sure I proved that during eight great years with Boro, during which time I played on the international stage too with the Republic of Ireland.

I had spells with Port Vale and Darlington at the end of my career, of course, before beginning a career in the media, commentating on Boro matches with Century, later to become Real Radio, and giving my views on the Three Legends show. I'm still on the airwaves today with my phone-in show on Community Voice FM and I'm back at the Boro as a matchday host in the Riverside Stadium's Legends Lounge.

I think the media work has a lot to do with my opinions. I've always had strong opinions and beliefs – I'll not be swayed by anybody. Whether you're a pauper or a king or a bigwig at a football club, it doesn't matter to me. You're not going to change my opinion. Whether I'm right or wrong I'll give my honest and forthright opinions and I think that's why I've lasted so long in the media.

I think the world is polluted by a politically correct brigade who want everyone to go by the book. Do me a favour! I've never gone by the book. I respect people – I'll respect everybody's opinion, but I won't always agree with them, simple as that.

People who don't know me probably think I'm arrogant, abrasive and confrontational. And, you know what? I can be! I am all of those things if you want me to be but I think I'm a good guy, a charitable guy. I'll help anybody, I think of other people and I don't believe I'm better than anyone else. But at the same time, I don't think anyone else is better than me. If I like someone it's not because of what their job is, what their title is or how much money they've got in the bank. If I like you, I like you.

So that's why I think I've managed to enjoy the career in the media that I have. On the pitch I achieved everything I wanted to and I'm proud to have been a success off it too. But, I have to say, it's been a rollercoaster ride. There have been plenty of ups but a fair few downs too during the last 30 years.

I joined Boro in 1985. I played two matches for the reserves on trial, the first a goalless draw at Grimsby and the second against Bradford at Ayresome Park which we won 4-2 and I was fortunate enough to score twice and set up the other two for my strike partner, Archie Stephens. The following morning I signed a two-year contract with an option of a further two years. I was delighted to sign on the dotted line because when I first came to England I was really excited at the prospect of playing for Middlesbrough. They were in the old Second Division, they had a big ground and decent support with it. It's 183 miles from Cliftonhill to Ayresome Park but it could have been a million miles, that's how big a difference it was. But that first year was a nightmare. We were relegated to Division Three and if we thought that was bad, we hadn't counted on what was to follow. The club went into liquidation in 1986, a lot of the players were shipped out, the manager who signed me - Willie Maddren - was sacked and it looked as if the club could disappear into oblivion. I couldn't believe it. I'd finally become a full-time professional footballer for a decent club and then the wheels came off completely.

However the manager who took over from Willie, Bruce Rioch, guided us from the Third Division to the First in consecutive years and for me that was a far greater achievement than Sir Alex Ferguson or Jose Mourinho winning the Premier League. Don't forget Bruce had a group of young lads, the majority born and bred in the area, and had no financial backing whatsoever after coming out of liquidation. In total I spent seven-and-a-half years at Middlesbrough and in that time I was fortunate enough to play 382 games, wearing the No 7 shirt for the vast majority of them. I won back-to-back Player of the Year awards in 1988 and 1989, I picked up the North-East Footballer of the Year trophy in 1990, and represented the Republic of Ireland and I was the club's top league scorer for six consecutive seasons. What gave me the most satisfaction, though, was the 1991/92 season when we won promotion to the first ever Premier League. I only played 26 games and although Paul Wilkinson beat me overall, I scored

THE REDS
FOOTBALL ACADEMY

Collectively our team have clocked up 1633 games wearing the red shirt of Middlesbrough FC, it's something we are all very proud of. Now our successful playing careers are over, we are looking to pass on our knowledge and experience that we have gained to help the youngsters reach their full potential.

Curtis Fleming Coach

Played 320 games in the red shirt of Middlesbrough FC, Republic of Ireland International, first team coach at Crystal Palace and Bolton, UEFA Pro licence holder.

Craig Hignett Coach

Played 200 games for Middlesbrough FC, assistant manager at Hartlepool and Middlesbrough FC, UEFA A licence holder.

Gary Pallister Director of Football

Made 250 appearances for Middlesbrough FC, spent nine successful years at Manchester United, England International.

Jim Platt Goalkeeping Coach

Former goalkeeper, played 481 games for Middlesbrough FC, manager of Darlington, Northern Ireland International, member of World Cup squad 1982, UEFA A licence holder.

Bernie Slaven Striking Coach

Made 382 appearances for Middlesbrough FC, scoring 147 goals, Republic of Ireland International, member of World Cup squad 1990, UEFA B licence holder.

To join Reds Academy or for more information contact us on:

Phone: 07403478998   Email: info@redsfa.co.uk   Twitter: @redsfa1

Fleming ——— Hignett ——— Pallister ——— Platt ——— Slaven ——

more than him in the league. All good things come to an end, though and I was forced out of the club by Lennie Lawrence, my last goal for Boro coming on October 3rd, 1992 in a 1-1 draw against Manchester United at Ayresome Park. That was my 147th goal for the club – not bad for a total unknown from north of the border who arrived from Albion Rovers for a fee of £25,000. To be the sixth top scorer in the club's 140-year history gives me an immense amount of pride and satisfaction. Only 10 Boro players have scored 100 goals or more for the club and to be in the illustrious company of Micky Fenton, George Camsell, Brian Clough, Wilf Mannion, Alan Peacock, David Mills, Billy Pease, George Elliott and John Hickton makes me feel privileged and as the only non-Englishman in that group I feel blessed.

A lot of people will look at footballers and probably mistakenly believe they earn a lot more money than they actually do and that they have the sort of glamorous life that the guy on the street could only dream about. But there are a lot of down sides to being a professional footballer too. I know because I've experienced them. Take a guy who does what you'd call an ordinary job – a shop assistant, an office clerk, a factory worker, anything like that. If he makes a boob at work he'll maybe get called to one side and given a slapped wrist from his boss and that's the end of it. But if a player makes a mistake on the pitch or a broadcaster gets it wrong on air, everyone's talking about it. There's no hiding place, especially these days. Before you know it, it'll be all over the internet and every Tom, Dick and Harry will be analysing it, scrutinising it and having his say on the matter.

The years that followed my playing days continued to be a turbulent ride. It's been peaks and troughs all the way, in every aspect. But I'm just like my late father in that I'm certainly not one for self-pity. That's not me. You won't catch me complaining that I've got it tough when the chips are down. The bottom line is that everyone has problems. But if you've got a problem, you can bet your life that there's a billion people in the world with problems bigger than yours! As I've said before, real pressure is when you've got four kids and you're on the dole so you can't afford to feed them. That's real pressure. So although I'd say there's pressure attached to being a professional footballer or a sports broadcaster, it's not in the same vein.

I've had some dark days and some experiences I've kept quiet about – until now – but when you read some of the things I've had to contend with, don't think I'm doing it out of self-pity because I'm not. I'm probably doing it more to try and help other people in the same situation.

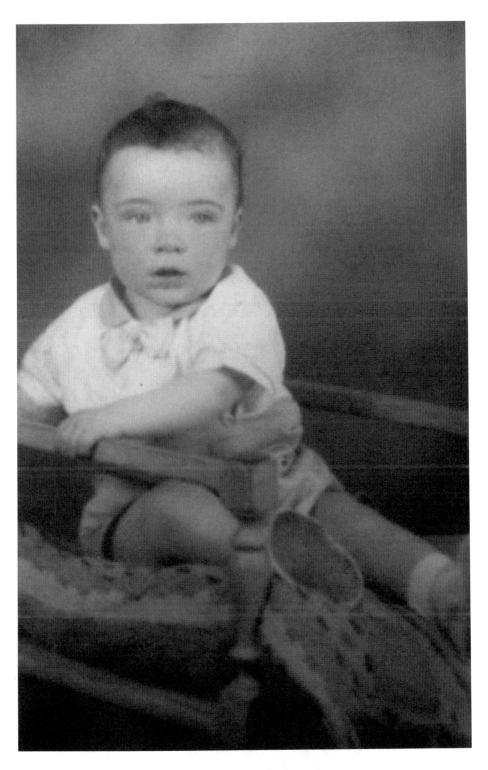

Pensive pose as a baby

Above with my ma Alice.

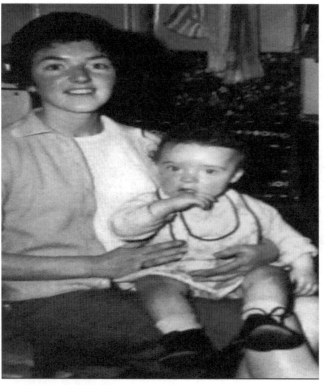

Left with my
favorite aunt
Kathleen

16 November spawned a monster

Early picture in Teesside.

Celebrating my first goal for Boro against Bradford

18 November spawned a monster

I'VE GOT TO
GO HOME

A NEW chapter in my life opened when I linked up with Malcol Macdonald and Eric Gates to do the Three Legends Show on Century Radio. It turned out to be the biggest radio phone-in show in the North-East, it ran for 14 years and our audiences were colossal. What's more, I was well suited to it because I was just the sort of opinionated ex-pro they needed.

It all started after Ali Brownlee and Bob Moncur did a show for Century in 1999 but, with the greatest of respect, it was light-weight compared to what we went on to achieve because neither of them had strong opinions or views. But on the back of that, Century invited me to a meeting at the Tall Trees in Yarm and announced they wanted to launch a show with me, Gary Rowell and Peter Beardsley. To do that, they would have to do away with Ali's show – but he was away at the time and knew nothing about it!

In the end it was me, Gatesy and Malcolm who made up the team and we went on to enjoy unprecedented success. The banter we had with fans and between ourselves was legendary and there wasn't even a sniff of club propaganda or bullshit. We said it exactly as it was.

But in the spring of 2007 the threesome that had worked so well for seven years was blown apart when Eric Gates was sacked. The amount of people who have asked over the years what happened to Gatesy is phenomenal, but the truth has never been revealed... until now. Here's what happened.

In March of that year, the Century Radio gaffer was a guy called John Myers and he requested to see me and Eric Gates at the station's HQ in Gateshead – but individually. He didn't want to see the two of us together. I went up to his top floor office at the appointed time and after being shown in, he came straight out with it and said "You've signed for the BBC haven't you?" Well, I was having none of it! In truth, the BBC were interested in taking over The Legends. After all, it was a hugely popular show right across the North-east. And yes, we'd had talks with them. We had even been offered a deal to jump ship but I wasn't going to tell Myers that.

The Century Radio top brass had obviously caught wind of what was going on but I just sat there, shrugged and protested "What do you mean I've signed for the BBC? Who told you that?" The truth of the matter was, though, that I already knew the answer to my own question. Only one person could have spilled the beans, and that was my Legends colleague Malcolm Macdonald. Myers wouldn't answer that one but he was adamant that I was up to no good and said to me "So if I go to the BBC and demand to see your pre-contract, your name won't be on it?" I told him that of course it wouldn't and that I'd signed nothing legally binding with anyone other than Century, it was as simple as that.

But he still wasn't happy. We had 18 months left on our contracts but he said that if things didn't improve in the studio, he'd have to make changes. The issue at the centre of it was that Malcolm and I weren't getting on and Myers told me it was quite clear from listening to the show that I wasn't responding to him. One example of that, apparently, was that Malcolm had read out a funny email on a recent show and I hadn't laughed. Well, that was nothing new! "To be honest, John," I told him, "I've never laughed at Malcolm."

Still he wouldn't give up and reckoned that we'd had some talk-ins lined up but failed to turn up as a threesome. The truth of it was that the previous week Gatesy and I had done one at Spennymoor with Ali Brownlee, my co-commentator on matchdays with Century. I wasn't going to skirt around the issue so I told Myers the blunt truth – we didn't want to work with Malcolm outside the radio studio. "It's your duty to promote the Three Legends under the Century banner," he retorted but I told him he'd got it wrong.

He'd been on the warpath throughout our meeting but suddenly the mood changed. Out of the blue he turned to me and said "I'd like to offer you an extension to your Legends contract." I didn't see that coming! Then at the end of the meeting he shook my hand and gave me a bear hug. Incredible.

So after I had my meeting I went to see Gatesy, whose turn it was next, and my advice to him was to keep his cool and deny everything. His meeting finished at 5.30pm and we were due to go on air at 6 o'clock. I fully expected him to be joining me in the studio as usual but as he came out he said to me "I've got to go home." He'd been shown the door.

That left me really confused, not to mention p***ed off, and I was even more surprised when I arrived at the studio for that evening's show to see Ali Brownlee there. He'd received a phone call from Century telling him they didn't expect me to turn up, so they wanted him to stand in for me. I told him he'd had a wasted journey up to Gateshead from Teesside and took my place in the studio.

I did the gig and quite honestly it was a nightmare. There was no way I was going to talk to Malcolm when we weren't on air and, in fact I didn't speak to him off air for a good five or six months. What really riled me that night was that instead of sitting opposite me as he'd always done, he sat next to me in Gatesy's seat. I couldn't believe it. What a cheek!

I was gutted to see Gatesy go, especially as I knew he wanted to carry on, but unlike me he was sacked. I was doing commentary on matchdays for Century as well, though, so I suppose that was the difference, although the Legends was the bigger show by far. It was at its peak at the time and we had more listeners than the Breakfast Show, which was unheard of.

So, for me at least, the show was continuing but I was more concerned about the commentary deal, because the deal for that was coming to an end at the same time and I needed to be at every Boro game to be able to do the Legends job properly. A few days after the meeting Myers sent me a text which read "Thanks for being a pro on Friday night. I appreciate it and we'll come back to you as soon as possible on the Boro deal contract extension as promised. BTW commentary was much better on Saturday."

The weeks rolled on and Myers reiterated that I had to get it right with Malcolm. He told me he didn't care if I didn't invite him to my next birthday party, or even the one after that, but we needed a rapport on air for the benefit of our listeners, and I agreed with that. What really rankled with me, though, was that it was Malcolm who had instigated the talks we'd had with the BBC in the first place. We'd all been offered contracts and the deal was that it was for a threesome. If there weren't three of us on board, the deal was off.

The three of us met with the BBC twice, the second time at the Malmaison Hotel on the Quayside in Newcastle where they gave us contracts. During the course of the meeting we were told that John Simons, who was Myers' right-hand man, had been in touch with the BBC and said "If you're interested in the Legends, you can have them." Did he mean it, though, or was that just a back-handed ploy to get us into trouble? I know what my answer would be!

So Gastesy signed his contract and I was on the verge of signing mine but Malcolm's was still in an envelope and he looked in no rush at all to put pen to paper. He appeared dishevelled, he hadn't shaved and looked as if he'd slept in a hedge all night. He looked like Catweazle! He was obviously disrupted and annoyed and he told us he needed more time to think about it, which meant Gatesy's signed contract wasn't valid because all three of us needed to do likewise.

The meeting finished early so Gatesy and I hung around there to have a chat before that night's Legends show, but Malcolm didn't join us. As the pair of us made our way to the studio, though, we spotted him coming over the Tyne Bridge from the Hilton hotel. There's no doubt he'd been in to see the gaffers and told them what had been going on.

As I've said before, I'm as honest and forthright as they come. If I've got a problem with someone I won't mess around, I'll have it out with them, and I always thought Malcolm was like that too. But I suppose he had a different background and a different up-bringing, he was a London boy, quite posh too, so maybe it was just a case of him dealing with things differently. But if he'd had a word with us first to tell us we had done something to annoy or upset him, that would have been a far better way of going about things. To disrupt the show when it was on such a high baffled me. I couldn't see his logic.

With no Gatesy we had a few weeks of having guests in to replace him before Micky Horswill was brought in to fill the gap permanently. And to be fair to Century, Malcolm and I were allowed to have a say in choosing his replacement. We needed someone knowledgeable, humorous and opinionated and we agreed on Micky. It was the first time we'd agreed on anything for a long time but my trust and bond with Malcolm had totally gone.

And what happened on the back of that was that Malcolm ended up on a different contract to me and was given an hourly slot doing No 9 interviews. We'd all been on the same money but after, shall we say, the dirty deed, it was as if he'd been rewarded for selling his soul. That p***ed me of greatly.

There was no point in confronting Malcolm about it because I knew what he'd done, He wasn't going to tell me anything I wasn't already aware of. But years later when I was working at Star Radio I saw a different side of Malcolm, a side I hadn't believed actually existed. He'd been very professional and invested money in Star and actually gave me money because I'd been out of pocket. Because of that I asked him if he'd been in to see the gaffer at Century to tell him what was going on and he admitted he had. Obviously I wanted to know why and he explained that when Gatesy signed his contract, he felt it was forcing him to do something he didn't want to. I realised then that it was something I'd probably overlooked too. But I still think Malcolm could have handled it in a better way.

I've always really liked Gatesy, he's a terrific guy and I kept in contact with him. He was still being paid for a time while he was off air and was made to sit by his phone every afternoon between half past four and half past five to wait for a call if they wanted him on the show. I kept in contact with him daily and visited him at his farm once a week, then one day about three or four weeks after he'd been shown the door he phoned me to say that Century been in touch to say they were contemplating putting him on the night shift. I asked him what on earth he'd be doing at that hour and he said "playing records". I couldn't stop laughing. I told him I could just imagine him playing all his favourite bands like Showaddywaddy and Mud!

I'll be honest, I still wanted to take the show to the BBC although it was obvious Malcolm wouldn't be part of it. We met Peter Beardsley, another Newcastle hero, a couple of times but he was involved in coaching young players at St James' Park. He would have needed permission from them to take on a broadcasting commitment and it didn't materialise. I also spoke to Chris Waddle but he already had a lot of other media commitments so that was another one off the list. Next on our hit list was John Anderson, who was already doing some work for the BBC at the time. He was keen to do it, but that didn't materialise either.

I was keen to do commentary for the BBC as well as taking the Legends there and we met a guy from the Boring Broadcasting Company as I call them, but he was far too pompous for my liking. He's quite probably a really nice guy but I took an instant dislike to him and it just didn't come off, which is a shame.

Now you might ask yourself why on earth I would want to work for a company I've just branded "boring" and you'd be right to raise that question. There are too many pundits who aren't just cheating themselves, but cheating their audiences too by just sitting on the fence and point blank refusing to give an opinion. If you want to hear a real pundit, listen to Roy Keane – in eight words he could say more than other so-called pundits could if they rambled on for 15 minutes. That's why I admire Roy and why I know I wouldn't have been any different on air if the BBC move had come off. When we had talks with the BBC, they were saying that they were trying to change their style – they wanted to hear more opinions and inject some more humour into their programmes, which would have been perfect for me, but it never really happened.

GOODBYE TO
THE LEGENDS

THE Three Legends was such a success because we had exactly the right chemistry. The arguments you heard on air were real, we were all passionate about our respective clubs and we would never shy away from fighting our own corner. As a result the listeners loved it. There were housebound or blind people who used to tune in and listening to the show was part of their life, an opportunity of a couple of hours' escapism every night. All good things come to an end, though, and so it proved with the Legends. There were behind the scenes changes and Century was rebranded Real Radio to fall in line with other stations which had been developed by the company, although at the time it was a case of 'carry on as normal' for us. But rumours were rife that another change was on the cards, this time involving Global Radio, whose stations included Capital and Heart. Sure enough the deal went through when Real Radio merged with Heart and this time it did affect us.

I'd been away to Australia and I was still jet-lagged when I was called into the Real Radio offices in Newcastle to be hit by the hammer blow. The show was being cancelled, our contracts were being terminated and we were out of a job. They also told us there would be a three-month silence clause during which we would still be paid. They were putting us out of a job and trying to gag us but I was having none of that and I said "You'll not silence me - I'll talk when I want to talk." It was like your missus telling you "I don't want you, pack your bags and get out," then as you're walking down the garden path she says "By the way, don't be going near another woman for another three months!" They didn't want us but they didn't want us speaking to anyone else, which just isn't on and I made my feelings on the matter clear in my weekly column in the Evening Gazette. It cost me money because I lost my severance pay as a result of speaking out but there's no way I was going to keep quiet on something like that. What I wrote in my column that day is reproduced below:

30 November spawned a monster

As you will have no doubt heard, the Three Legends show has been axed.

After 13 years of record-breaking radio shows that have put bums on seats across the region and brought in lord knows how much in advertising cash, myself, Micky Horswill and Malcolm Macdonald have been given the elbow.

That's cruel. Obviously we are all very disappointed because we loved doing the job and all think we were doing it well.

It was a real shock, not least because me and Micky were still jet-lagged. We had barely touched down after a holiday in Australia when we got called into the offices in Newcastle and were told that's it, your contracts are terminated as of now. Welcome back to England. Thanks and goodbye.

We've made our opinions known to the station chiefs as you can imagine but it is a done deal. We're out.

And it is not because of audience figures, whatever the official statement says. Real Radio announced on their website that was the reason. And yes, our figures were down measured against the massive highs of when we first started 13 years ago - but radio audiences have gone down right across the industry. You can only measure us on the audiences we get now and in our time slot and in our region right now there is nobody even close to us.

Check out the RAJAR figures. The Three Legends is still the number one show on the Real Radio network right across the country, just as we were when it was Century Radio. The Three Legends is the number one show of any type and in any time slot in the region on commercial or the BBC. And the Three Legends is the number one show in the whole country in the 6-8pm slot. We have more listeners than TalkSport, Five Live and any show on any local station you care to name. We delivered.

So yes, we had dipped from the record breaking highs of 10 years ago - but we're still top. And the statement said the decline in audience was partly down to social media - but we were bang up to date with that technology. We were quick to build readers e-mails, then Facebook, then Twitter into the show. We were getting the best out of social media. The station chiefs were delighted.

But hey, it is a cut-throat world. We know that. We've all been in football. And radio is no different to a lot of other industries right now that are making cuts, rationalising and downsizing and getting rid of staff and making changes that don't suit the customer but only suit the money men.

Real is being bought out by Capital Radio who own half of the commercial radio in the UK. What we do doesn't suit what they do which is wall to wall chart music like Adele and Rhianna. It's cheap to make, can be done nationally and it's aimed at a younger and mainly female audience. I don't think we three old guys will fit in.

So we are out. Sometimes it doesn't matter how well you do your job, if the big picture changes, you're out.

And it's happened before to me. It reminds me of when I was doing commentary on the Boro with Ali Brownlee. I had done 500 plus games with the station and we'd just won some big international broadcasting industry award in New York for our work following Boro to the UEFA Cup final - then we had the plug pulled on us! And they say lightning doesn't strike twice!

My biggest regret is not being able to say goodbye to the brilliant and loyal audience we have built up over the years.

I can't say how genuinely I mean that. I know the show has its knockers and a lot of people don't like it - but hundreds of thousands of football fans across the North-east do. They love it. They love to listen and they love to take part. And that is what has made the show such a success: the listeners; the people who call in or e-mail, or tweet, or stop us in the street and give us their opinion on their team. There have been plenty of football shows. Any ex-player can talk about the game. But what made the Legends was the interplay with listeners.

I think the three of us have big personalities and big opinions and you get no club propaganda or bull from any of us. We call it as we see it and sometimes that upsets people but we are all honest blokes we care about our clubs. But more importantly we also know what football is really about: it's about the fans. It's about how supporters feel about their team, how your emotions change from week to week depending on the result and it's about good natured banter between rivals. We encouraged all those things with the listeners. We encouraged callers to tease each other and us too. We dished it out and we could take it too. We made it fun and people responded. The show developed a life of its own with the theme tunes and catchphrases and the wind-ups.

That is why it broke records for audience figures and why other people tried to copy it. They rolled the format out across the Century and Real Radio networks in a lot of different regions and even the BBC in Teesside and Tyneside tried their own versions but no-one got within a mile of us.

So it is very, very disappointing that something that was being enjoyed by so many people has been scrapped so suddenly. It was a great show to do. And there's still plenty of mileage in a show like that - and there will be so long as passionate fans in this region care about their club.

So, believe me, you haven't heard the last of us. Boro fans definitely haven't heard the last of Bernie Slaven. No way.

I hope we can do something in some shape or form to keep the Three Legends alive. We are talking over a few ideas at the moment and you can be sure that whatever happens Boro fans will be the first to know via the Evening Gazette and my website.

Watch this space.

I lost my three months' money because of that but it had to be said. And whether I opened my mouth or kept it closed, it made no difference. That was it. Finished. After 13 years of top figures we were no longer no wanted.

The statement the radio station put out about the cancellation of the Legends was wishy washy drivel:

"Due to the explosion of social media, this type of content is widely available on many platforms whenever and wherever people want it. While we appreciate our sports shows had a small but passionate following, in-depth sports programming is not something that appeals to the majority of our audience and, over time, we have been reducing the level of sports related broadcasts on the station. We will be replacing the Legends sports show with music programming that has broad appeal to our audience. This will be mixed with travel, news, weather and showbiz to aid the drive home. Our news service will continue to deliver relevant sports news throughout the day."

So there you have it. The way I saw it was that the prospective new owners of the station didn't want us so they had all the dirty work done before the takeover. I can't prove that, obviously, but it's certainly what it smacked of. For me, what the statement should have said is that they were being bought out, they were under strict orders to clear the decks for the rebranding of Real to Heart, which has since happened, and when the new owners were in place and the flak started flying they could say "It's nothing to do with us." They shouldn't have tried to bullshit everyone and, if you ask me, their statement should also have included "We're ripping the heart out of local content and we're going to be networking everything from London and Manchester. Instead of the Three Legends we're going to play Adele and Rhianna every night." To my mind that would have been telling it like it was.

I also believe that Century were a wee bit embarrassed about our success. We had higher audience figures than the Breakfast Show and we were still going strong after all those years but we weren't their baby. They'd inherited us from station's previous bosses. It's like when a manager of a football club signs a new player and discovers that someone the previous gaffer brought in is doing a better job. Because of the takeover talk we weren't altogether surprised by the decision but it was a blow nonetheless.

On the face of it, that was the end of the Three Legends. Even though we'd had talks with them in the past the BBC wouldn't touch us because by then they had their own show called Total Sport with Marco Gabbiadini and John Anderson, but I wasn't so sure it was the end and I still believed something would happen to keep us together on air.

And I was right. We took the show to Star Radio in Darlington although that didn't cater for our entire audience which was spread right across the North-East so Malcolm and I visited every one of the local community radio stations to see if we could get them involved and we did really well. Koast Radio and Community Voice FM took the show along with several others. Modern technology allowed the younger members of our audience to listen to us on their smartphones, which was a great boost for us, and the older generation could continue listening on their radios.

But the biggest problem we had was that we weren't getting paid. Malcolm shelled out the cash for me for three months and the radio station paid us a wee bit, but the idea had always been that their marketing team would pull in some sponsorship money, put it in a pot to share out and we would all be happy. It was the biggest radio show in the North-east, surely there would be no shortage of companies keen to get involved? That's what you would have thought but over a course of the year the number of sponsors they managed to attract amounted to zilch. They couldn't find a single one, or so they told us, anyway. There were 40 adverts throughout our show – 26 individual adverts plus 14 repeats – but still we didn't get a penny from them.

Once we'd been told there was no-one prepared to put any money in, we knew we couldn't stay at Star and that was us out of the door. We continued with the Legends on Koast and CVFM but the money was minimal. We'd been on very good money at Real Radio, we were earning thousands of pounds between us every month, and I was on a decent wage for doing the commentary too, so it was quite a comedown. I've never been driven by cash although you do need it to survive of course, and with sponsorship money in short supply these days, we took the agonising decision to say goodbye to the Three Legends once and for all in 2014.

It was a unique show with a winning formula. When Gatesy left Micky Horswill came in with a dry sense of humour and some great stories to tell even if he wasn't as opinionated as me or Malcolm, and Dickie Ord was a good addition to although he joined us near the end of the Three Legends' run and he didn't get a fair crack of the whip really.

We used to send each other up all the time and whenever we did any talk-ins, Micky would always introduce Malcolm as "the clever one". But that would be the cue for me to question it by saying "Clever? He's had four wives, 12 kids, he's been bankrupt and an alcoholic… and he played for Newcastle! If that makes him clever, I must be a f***ing genius!"

I still think the Three Legends could work if we had the opportunity. The ingredients came together by chance but they were all there. The balance was spot on – Malcolm was the pompous headmaster with me and Gatesy the two schoolkids. Had we run our course? Well if the audience figures had dropped dramatically before our contracts were terminated I would have to admit that we had, but that wasn't the case.

Sunderland Legend changes again this time we pose with Dicky Ord.

BANKRUPTCY

BEING a pundit on Century Radio was a dream job for me. I'd taken the place of Malcolm Allison, the larger than life former Boro manager, who had been shown the door after calling a linesman "a f***ing disgrace" live on air having already been suspended once before for swearing, and I thoroughly enjoyed the experience as well as being one half of a double act with Ali Brownlee, who taught me the ropes.

I have to be honest, being on the radio didn't come naturally to me. Someone from the studio will be talking into your ear while you're describing the on-pitch action and concentrating on what is going on – there's so much going on that sometimes in your early days you can get tongue-tied when your brain knows what you want to say but your mouth doesn't get the message. But Ali was always there to help me out.

What I did find about being on the radio was that often if you made a comment about an individual or a team, it would be passed on by about 20 people before reaching them and by that time it bore no resemblance to what you'd said. It could be like a game of Chinese whispers, so I always made it clear that if anyone had a problem, all they had to do was come and see me. Strangely enough, nobody ever did come and see me though.

I had some great times commentating, especially as it coincided with a golden age for Boro. I was there in the commentary box for the three cup finals at Wembley, that famous Carling Cup victory over Bolton at the Millennium Stadium, Cardiff, in 2004, two European campaigns and the UEFA Cup final in 2006. Since I stopped doing commentary they haven't come close to repeating that, so I must have been a lucky charm! I thought I'd done well by playing 382 games for Middlesbrough but to achieve more than 500 as a summariser was something else. I'm really proud of that.

One of the highlights was Boro's amazing comeback against Steaua Bucharest in the second leg of their UEFA Cup semi-final. It looked all over for Gareth Southgate and the boys until an incredible late turnaround sent the Romanians crashing out and Boro into the final at Eindhoven's Philips Stadion. Remember that dramatic headed goal by Massimo Maccarone? Who could forget it? Ali Brownlee was so excited he invited everyone on Teesside round to his house for a party and a parmo! That commentary, along with the big game previews and post-match interviews earned us the Best Sports Coverage award at the New York Radio Festival, another amazing honour. But just a few short months after Ali and I had been over to the Big Apple to collect our award, we lost the commentary. That, in my opinion was farcical.

The bottom line is that Century had previously shared the commentary rights with BBC Radio Cleveland (now BBC Tees) for several years but for what they called "commercial reasons" Boro decided to award exclusive rights to one station for the 2007-8 season… and it wasn't us. I heard a number of reasons why Century didn't get the contract – that it was down to finances, that the club was holding out for more money, that it was down to my opinions. Which one was right is anyone's guess, although I wouldn't be too surprised if the reason was to do with money. That said, I don't think the club was too disappointed to see me go. I've always maintained that all I did was give my opinions on what I saw, it's not as if I was on the radio telling the listeners not to buy a season ticket or demanding they stay away from games! Ali of course went to the BBC to front their matchday commentary team but I was still doing the Legends show on Century so our partnership came to an end.

Debbie Bowman, the station's managing director, put out a statement at the time to the listeners. It read:

"It is disappointing after 12 years not to be involved in the Middlesbrough commentary next season and also on a personal level for Ali Brownlee as it would have been his 25th year of commentary and for Bernie, who with Ali, won the Gold Award at the New York Festival Awards and completed their 500th commentary last season. It was our intention to broadcast all three North-East Premiership football commentaries next season, which would have delivered incisive commentary to all fans across the region. We wanted to continue to deliver the commentary but at the end of the day, the club has announced they are doing an exclusive deal with the BBC. We wish the club well and pledge our continued support to the club and the fans. Just because Century fm will not be broadcasting the commentary next season, it doesn't mean our commitment to the club and the fans is in any way diminished."

During the build-up to the start of the season the radio station asked me and Ali to go along to the Riverside Stadium and pose for publicity photographs in Boro shirts. I didn't want to do it because it was looking more and more likely I wouldn't be commentating on the club any more, but Ali talked me into it. Sure enough we didn't get the deal and the pictures never saw the light of day. Even though I knew we should never have agreed to the photoshoot and I'd seen what was going to happen, it was still a big blow to lose the commentary and the fans seemed to see it that way too. We had the right balance, with me and Ali it was like good cop, bad cop, and even though he was often accused of looking at things through Boro-tinted spectacles and I was supposedly too critical, it was a winning formula with the fans. I've kept a welter of emails sent in by supporters after it was announced our partnership was breaking up and here is a small selection of them:

"Gutted by the news, guess this is how the club reward loyalty."

"I am very disappointed at the decision even though I am a Sunderland supporter. I have always tuned in to Ali and Bernie whenever their game has not clashed with ours. I really enjoyed their style of commentary and I will miss their show a great deal."

"Please pass my thanks on to Bernie and Ali for the years of brilliant commentating on Boro matches. I am gutted that I will no longer be able to sit back on match days knowing I will get plenty of laughs and passion, it will never be the same. I have expressed my disgust to the MFC website but what good does that do at the end of the day?"

"DEVASTATED!!! Ali, Bernie and Century were the voice of the Boro. I am disappointed that MFC have decided to 'honour' Ali's 25th year of commentary in such an underhand way."

"Just a note to say I think it is an absolute travesty that the best commentary team on radio will not be Century commentating on Boro's games next season. They should quickly be seconded by another radio station and thereby attract lots more listeners and supporters!"

"It's sad to see you and Ali won't be doing any more Boro commentary. This means I don't have an excuse to get out of going shopping with the wife or watching Coronation Street and EastEnders. I respect that you say things how you see them and don't take any notice of fickle Boro fans who don't like the truth."

And there's plenty more where that little lot came from. The fans were clearly not happy and to start with I was gutted at losing the commentary too. I loved the involvement, I loved going to the games and I loved giving my opinions on them. Ali and I would always be at the ground at one o'clock and we'd still be in our seats way after the final whistle had blown so the days were long but incredibly enjoyable. My old mate Gatesy used to tell me I was off my head and although I really missed doing it to start with, as the months rolled on and the cold winter weather arrived, I realised he was right. I remember going to Tottenham for a match one evening. It was a freezing cold night and we didn't leave the ground until gone 11.30, then on the way back the car blew up so we didn't arrive home until around 8 o'clock the next morning! You don't get any extra money or any more thanks when that happens so at least nights like that were all a thing of the past.

Unfortunately also a thing of the past was the money I was getting for doing the commentary. The total amount I lost over a season was £24,000 which included quarterly bonuses and losing the deal was the start of a terrible time for me financially. I'd bought a plot of land in Thirsk, three acres in total, with the intention of building a house on it. I'd bought it at an auction and paid £270,000 for it which was way over the odds for it to start with. The people selling it must have thought I was mad. The only dwelling on the land when I bought it was a rotten old wooden shack with no electricity or running water so for a year and a half I stayed in a second hand caravan on the land with my dogs while I knocked it down and built what I'd intended to be a lovely new house to move into.

As it turned out, the whole project was an absolute nightmare from start to finish. Planning permission was refused twice by Hambleton Council although I can assure you I wasn't trying to build Buckingham Palace or the Taj Mahal, I just wanted a decent-sized house to live in with three or four bedrooms. There was so much red tape to cut through it was unbelievable and after having two planning applications thrown back at me, I ended up having to build half the house underground to comply with the regulations.

Of course to build a house you need an architect and they don't come cheap. Mine certainly didn't, even though I only saw him once on site, standing in a muddy field wearing a suit I'd have put on for a wedding and a dapper pair of smart shoes. His fee ended up double what it was going to be as a result of the refused planning applications and the work needed to find a way of getting the house built.

The builder came highly recommended by a friend and it took him and his team just under a year to do the job. During that time a group of builders came every day and worked non-stop until just before the end of the build when there were just a few minor alterations left to be carried out, and they started to appear less frequently. That was fair enough because we were almost done, or so I thought! One day I walked into the master bedroom, which was in the basement, and when I went to close the door I discovered it had jarred. On closer inspection of the floor I noticed it had swelled so I immediately contacted the builder to come over and when he did, he discovered two feet of water under the floorboards.

After six months of investigation there was still no solution and by that time I realised I would have to sell the new house because of the amount it was costing me. I was desperate to get the house on the market after spending so much money on it and losing a large part of my income so I ended up employing a tanking firm to waterproof the basement and install a pump. The work was done effectively and efficiently within four weeks but the problem was cost – I had to shell out £13,000 to have it done. It was money I didn't have because I was struggling financially but I couldn't sell the house without having the work done so it was a Catch 22 situation so I had to borrow the money from a friend.

It seemed clear to me that the builder had tried to cut corners regarding the tanking and that the reason I had water coming through the floorboards was a result of his poor workmanship. In hindsight I could see he should have hired a specialist company. I set about attempting to retrieve the £13,000 from him but when he refused point blank to pay me, I had no option but to take him to court in Middlesbrough. On the day of the hearing I received a phone call from my solicitor to say he had settled.

At last I had a house I could sell, albeit because I was being forced to, and I had it valued at the grand sum of £775,000, so for a quick sale I dropped the asking price by £25,000. But guess what? No sooner had I put it up for sale than the property market collapsed for the first time in ten years. Great – just when things had started finally looking up, another kick in the teeth. After two months without any interest I dropped the asking price further to £650,000 and employed a second estate agent but still there was little interest and by that time I was starting to slip below the waterline and I was receiving phone calls from Lloyds Bank regarding the mortgage arrears. Down came the asking price again to £599,000 and then to £525,000 but still I couldn't shift it. A year passed and by that time Lloyds were on the phone to me every other day but I'd hit a dead end. I didn't know where to go, who to turn to or what to do but my mate Gatesy put me in touch with some friends who had experienced similar circumstances. They calmed me down, put things into perspective and advised me what to do. As you can imagine, it was all a very unpleasant experience but I kept telling myself that it wasn't going to kill me and that I still had my kids. That's what kept me sane.

After talking to Gatesy and his mates my first port of call was John McQueen, founder of the Bankruptcy Association and after that I began to see the light at the end of the tunnel. If anyone reading this is going through something similar, I'd urge you to do the same. This guy will sort you out. The first piece of advice I was given was that the only sensible way forward was to declare myself bankrupt and after a discussion with John, my mind was set on going down that route. I was put in touch with an insolvency solicitor, who by coincidence worked in office next to Real Radio, and he told me straight that it was just a matter of time before I declared myself bankrupt.

In the meantime I sat back and let Lloyds take me to court in Darlington with regards to my mortgage arrears. When I arrived in court for my hearing it was like a cattle market, there were hundreds of people crammed into one room with no privacy whatsoever and when it was your turn to go into the courtroom your name was blasted out for all to hear. If I'm honest, it was embarrassing and degrading. I was given a month to sell the property or I would have to return for another hearing, which was the outcome I had expected.

In the meantime I was advised to look for a rented property to live in and strip the existing one bare, not leaving so much as a light bulb, as I wouldn't get a better price for it if I did. A few days later I decided to face up to the inevitable - I walked into Lloyds Bank in Stockton and asked to see the manager. When he appeared he assumed I was there to pay the money I owed them but he was wrong. I placed my house keys on his desk and told him "The problem is now yours, I'm walking away from it". His immediate response was that he wasn't sure if he could accept them but after going off to check he issued me a receipt for the keys and that was it, the house now belonged to them. But instead of feeling depressed at losing my home, I felt as if I had lifted the World Cup! I was relieved and it gave me a great sense of satisfaction to be in control of the situation.

Not long after handing the keys in I received an official letter from Lloyds to confirm that they had repossessed the house and just before Christmas that year I heard from them again, this time to inform me that they had sold it for £325,000 – less than half of the valuation I'd first been given. They also pointed out that I still owed them £200,000 and wanted to know how I would like to pay the outstanding balance. Clearly I was in no position to be able to pay that sort of sum so Christmas passed and in the New Year I gathered as much information as I possibly could about bankruptcy. In mid-February I went to Teesside Magistrates Court in Middlesbrough and asked for a court hearing to declare myself bankrupt.

Celebrating 500 commentary games with Ali Brownlee.

IT'S NOT
ALL DOOM
AND GLOOM

LEADING up to my first bankruptcy hearing on March 31st 2010, I had to fill in all sorts of forms – they even wanted to know what my shoe size was and what colour underpants I was wearing! Well not quite, but I had to supply so much information that I wouldn't have been surprised if they had wanted to know. But the most bizarre thing of all was that even though I was declaring myself bankrupt I had to pay £450 for the privilege, although if Lloyds Bank had forced the issue, I wouldn't have had to part with a penny.

On the morning of the hearing, which took place at Teesside Magistrates Court in Middlesbrough, I put on my pin-striped suit which I had bought from Oxfam, polished my shoes and made sure I was at court for 8.30am as I'd been told they operated on a first come first served basis and I certainly didn't want to be there any longer than I had to. When I entered the court building I had a brief chat with two security guards who body searched me, although the conversation we had was obviously about football and not bankruptcy. As I entered the reception area I was stood in darkness but at nine o'clock the lights came on and someone arrived to take my £450 off me along with my bankruptcy papers and I was asked to sign a form and swear on oath, which I did, before being shown next door to a room full of lawyers, barristers and members of the public. After half an hour a lady shouted my name out and led me out of the busy room, along a corridor into the judge's chambers where a judge awaited my arrival. As I walked in the first things I noticed were a large oak table and six chairs with the judge sitting at a desk at the very end. I sat down the judge said to me "I thought I'd get you in here first before the crowds" and after looking at my files he was in agreement with my decision, and reassured me that it wasn't all doom and gloom.

Declaring myself bankrupt was obviously a big step to take but the judge told me to bear three points in mind – one, I was free of debt; two, I wouldn't have to deal with any of the creditors; and three, I'd be out of it in a year. He stamped my bankruptcy papers and as I got up and walked towards the door he said "Hey, it could have been worse. I'm a Sunderland fan, I could have been a Geordie!" After a couple of years of uncertainty, turmoil and stress it was all over in five minutes.

The form I'd been given by the judge had to be taken back to the reception area where the hard-nosed cow behind a desk bawled out "Mr Slaven!" That was the worst part of the whole experience. The last thing you want after coming through a humiliating experience is some jumped up office clerk trying to degrade you even more by shouting out your name for all and sundry to hear, I hope one day she finds herself in similar circumstances and then she'll know how you're made to feel in a situation like that.

Three days after doing the dirty deed I flew to Marbella in Spain – not bad after being made bankrupt – to be with my youngest son, Ryan, who was representing Marton Hall Drive in a football tournament, and during that four-day break my mind was relieved of the pressure of bankruptcy. To raise my mood even more, the team won the tournament.

A few days after my return I had a meeting with the Official Receivers in Stockton above the DVLA office. I took my plastic stacker boxes filled to the brim with bills, documents, bank statements, radio contracts and anything else I could lay my hands on that I thought they would want to see. I'd been warned in advance that this was going to be the most difficult part of the whole process and I was shown to a small private room where two officers from the Insolvency Service spent two and a half hours quizzing me and grilling be about how I got into financial difficulties. These guys told me they were filling in for David H Storry who had locked the Ayresome Park gates back in the dark days of Middlesbrough's liquidation crisis in 1986. One of the two guys suggested I should sign a photograph of him padlocking the gates but I just looked at him and told him to f*** off!

In fairness, though, the two of them were ultra-professional. They were full of questions and left no stone unturned in their mission to find out the background to my financial troubles but at the same time they were fair and made me feel at ease. Every time a question was asked they would delve into my plastic box and find a document to back up my story. At the end of the meeting one of the guys told me that the story hadn't seemed to stack up at the start but they were now satisfied that everything had been clarified as to why I had ended up in that mess.

Probably not a lot of people know this, but when in bankruptcy you are allowed to have a job and earn a wage, which was great for me as I was still doing the Three Legends show. The procedure is that anything you earn after a year, minus living expenses, has to be paid to the Official Receiver for three years in monthly pay-ments. I was fortunate to receive a substantial amount of money for my radio work so I was in a good position and after filling out a form detailing my living expenses which included three dogs, a pony, a goat and two cats to feed, I ended up paying £450 a month, which was less than I initially thought it would be. What I hadn't expected, though, was that the Insolvency Service discovered I had an undisclosed asset. No it wasn't a Rolls Royce, not a villa in Spain, not a luxury yacht but in fact my ten-year-old Shetland pony! As a result I received a letter telling me that if I wished to keep the pony I'd have to pay £100. Needless to say I sent off a cheque without hesitation, although if it had been the goat I might have had to think more carefully!

While deciding which way to go with regard to declaring bankruptcy, one of my biggest concerns was my radio job as I'd looked through my contract and discovered there was a clause which said anyone declared bankrupt could have their employment terminated at the station's discretion. On realising that I immediately went to see Debbie Bowman, the MD, and two days later she phoned me with the good news that it wouldn't be a problem. In between that meeting and declaring bankruptcy I was handed a new two-year contract but I refused to sign it because the same clause was included. I've always believed you should never sign a contract you're not happy with and never settle for a verbal agreement. A couple of weeks later, however, I was given a different version with the clause removed and I was happy to put pen to paper this time.

Although declaring bankruptcy was down to my own individual circumstances, I was far from alone in being in that situation. Thousands of people already knew what it felt like, among them former Blackburn and Scotland striker Colin Hendry, Sunderland FA Cup winner Bobby Kerr and ex-Boro and Newcastle midfielder Irving Natress. Even my radio colleagues Micky Horswill and Malcolm Macdonald have been through it, and it had me wondering whether we should change the name of our show to the Three Bankrupts! The list goes on and the majority of the high profile names had appeared in media. Thankfully mine never came to light although one day while I was on the internet I was shocked to read the headline 'Bernie bankrupt' on the Google search engine just below my own official website. My first thought was "Oh no, it's out," and even though I was dreading having to read the article, I gritted my teeth and clicked on it. And when the story appeared on my screen I was ecstatic to discover it was an article referring to when Middlesbrough went bankrupt in 1986 and I was among the players affected. Phew!

Malcolm actually advised me to try and go to London to have the case heard – that way it could potentially get lost in the system and people in the North-East would be none the wiser about what was going on. When we were doing the Legends we were high profile and Malcolm's reasoning was that the press were more likely to find out about it if it was heard locally and, if they did, they'd have a field day. Malcolm and Micky Horswill had both had brushes with the law which made it into the press, so he was talking from experience. I was more concerned about how the news of my bankruptcy would affect my family than how it would affect me personally so I made some enquiries and it turned out that I couldn't have had it heard down there anyway because I had a North-east postcode. As it happened it didn't matter anyway because the story never became public knowledge but I appreciated Malcolm trying to help me nevertheless. I was fortunate enough to benefit from a lot of good advice and guidance and Eric Gates was a help too. He came along to support me at my hearing in Darlington and he let me store a lot of my belongings in a barn at his farm in Easington while I was looking for somewhere to live because I had nowhere else to put them. Some years earlier he'd done the same for former Sunderland captain and FA Cup winner Bobby Kerr, so that shows what sort of guy he is.

I was going to come clean on the air one night on the Legends show and reveal I was bankrupt but Jon Kirby, the controller, advised me to keep it quiet. I'm being open about it now because it can happen to anybody at any time – you don't have to lose millions to be declared bankrupt, it can happen for the sake of as little as £1,000. It could happen to a husband and father who has lost his job so suddenly there's no money coming in to pay the mortgage. He and his family then face losing the house so everybody is at risk of being uprooted. That's the sort of effect it can have.

I was in a fairly comfortable position, though, because I still had money coming in but it's so sad what can happen overnight and you're powerless to do anything. OK I have to take some of the rap as well for the position I ended up in but the property market crashing wasn't my fault! I maybe borrowed more than I should have done, but shouldn't the bank take some responsibility for allowing it to happen by lending me so much in the first place? I was fortunate enough to still be working on the radio, so I had an income.

I received money from the Boro Former Players' Association when I was struggling financially although I took it reluctantly as there were – and still are – players worse off than me, despite my predicament at the time. Thankfully I got myself back on the right track and it's all behind me now.

With Marton Hall Drive coaches and my son Ryan in Majorca, I flew out just after declaring bankruptcy.

In order to keep my only asset. I paid £100 for my pony.

DEPRESSION

AFTER the house was repossessed I moved into rented accommodation in Newton Under Roseberry but, to be honest, even if I had a magnificent job and earned a boatload of money I still wouldn't buy a house again. Not unless I could walk into the estate agents, slap a big wad of cash on the table and pay for it outright, anyway, because it's just a noose around your neck. In certain parts of Europe they don't believe in mortgages and I can certainly see why. Nobody is guaranteed a job for life so you could suddenly find yourself being unable to afford to pay what you owe and it's so unfair that a family could be booted out of their home because their circumstances have changed.

I don't know what can be done, but I really think there should be something in place to safeguard people like that.

It was a bleak time for me as I battled to overcome my financial problems but it wasn't just my pocket that was affected, it was my mental health too. The first time I ever felt low and depressed was back in 1988 during my playing days when I hit a barren spell in front of goal. Nothing felt right in January and February of that year and after banging in the goals for Middlesbrough I went through a drought. The form I was in, I couldn't have hit the main stand, let alone the back of the net. It wasn't just out on the pitch either, it was in training too - I just didn't want to be there. It even crossed my mind to pack in playing professional football, which would have been a massive decision for me, especially as I had worked so hard to get where I was in the first place.

It became obvious to some of those around me that I wasn't in a good place and I received a handwritten letter from my cousin Caroline, who was a teacher, encouraging me to get back to my old self. Bruce Rioch, who was manager of Boro at the time, was aware that I was struggling in front of goal and that I had lost my confidence but he didn't know exactly how bad how much it was affecting me.

We played Aston Villa at Ayresome Park live on TV and while we were having our pre-match meal at a hotel in County Durham, Bruce called me over to his table. I was convinced he was going to tell me I was dropped, and I wasn't the only one who thought I wouldn't be playing because the local and national media as well as my team-mates shared that opinion. But instead of leaving me out, Bruce told me "I believe in you and once you get that elusive goal, you'll be back." As it turned out I didn't score but Boro won 2-1, I set up Alan Kernaghan for one of the goals and Bruce praised me in the press afterwards. As a result my confidence started to come back.

Thankfully that was the only time in my football career I was affected by depression and it was slight, but it did however return and in a much stronger form. In 2010 and 2011 I was going through a divorce from my wife Karen, had my house in North Yorkshire repossessed and I was made bankrupt. All of this took its toll.

Before Christmas 2010 I realised I had to really focus to hold a conversation and sometimes even then it didn't feel real – it was like a dream. By January my self-esteem was very low and I started worrying about everything. Even since my playing days finished I'd always liked to keep myself fit but I stopped training, sleeping became difficult and I lost my appetite for a couple of weeks. I found it a struggle to get up in the mornings, I felt nervy and very uneasy, although despite my condition I still managed to do a week-long coaching course in Sunderland with Micky Horswill. How I got through that I will never know, I didn't want to be there and all the time I was there I just wanted to run away. I continued to do the Legends show which became unbelievably difficult because I had no control, drive or energy and quite honestly it felt like I was dying. But the worst symptom was that I wanted to run away, for instance I was waiting at a garage for my tyres to be changed when I just disappeared. I returned later to collect my car but I still felt terrible.

During that two-week period I was in the Metro Centre having a coffee with some friends but I just couldn't drink it and I couldn't fathom what was wrong with me. Despite being a music lover I was no longer switching on the radio or playing any of the CDs that I would normally enjoy listening to and eventually it got to the stage where I knew I had to do something. I booked a couple of sessions with a hypnotherapist called Jean Brady at Park View Clinic in Marton. She helped me when I went to see her about my fear of flying so I decided to see if she turn things round for me this time. I had several sessions there and during my visits I put on a blindfold, listened intently and talked about positive things like beaches, birds and forests. It might sound strange but it really worked.

Until now I have never discussed my problems with depression. It may have been brief but it was very personal and mentally disturbing. I would never have thought that I was someone who could be affected by depression but nobody is bulletproof from it and it can strike at any time.

During the time I was suffering from it I preferred to be alone than be in company and I used to sit in my car outside the studio until it was time to go on air because I couldn't face talking to the lads. It was the weirdest sensation but I never revealed how I was feeling and hopefully I managed to hide it from the listeners because they would have had their own problems and certainly wouldn't want to hear about mine.

Eventually I went to see my doctor. Before my appointment I was given a questionnaire to fill in – there were ten questions in all and I answered 'yes' to nine of them. The only one I answered 'no' to was "Do you want to kill yourself?" That was the most important one but even so nine out of ten was pretty compelling evidence and as I walked back to my car and sat down in the driver's seat I shed a tear and said to myself "It's official – I'm a loon."

I was prescribed Citalopram but my appetite remained low to start with. I remember one night having bacon, eggs, beans and fried bread put in front of me but, as delicious as it looked, as soon as it touched my lips I wanted to bork. I took the tablets for six months but during that time I continued to be restless in bed, continued to worry and still broke out in hot and cold sweats. I returned to training however, and although it started to get easier, going on runs at first I felt heavy-legged, my breathing was erratic and I found my mind wandering. Once I started to get back into my stride, though, I began to notice a difference.

The first sports star I ever heard about suffering from depression was Marcus Trescothick and since then Mike Yardy, his fellow England cricketer, has also been treated for it. So too has Neil Lennon, the former Celtic manager and official figures tell us that nearly one in five adults will suffer from depression at some point during their life. It could affect literally anyone. In 2012 former Middlesbrough player Dean Windass went public and discussed his mental issues – now I know Dean, I've played in five-a-side tournaments with him and commentated with him and he's always struck me as a mentally strong, tough as old boots character but his condition was so severe that he twice attempted to take his own life. And one day in November 2011 I was signing books and DVDs at the Metro Centre with Malcolm Macdonald and Micky Horswill when a middle-aged man approached us and told us that Gary Speed, the former Leeds and Wales star, had died. The three of us were totally shocked and stunned at the tragic news and when I looked on my iPhone I discovered Gary had hanged himself. The following evening I read a few Tweets from a lad I used to work with called Adam Lindsey and one of them read *"Gary Speed's death has made me think a lot and reassess how I've been going about things for years."* He posted more comments about mental health issues still carrying a stigma, which forced most sufferers to hide from them in order to avoid being judged because of them, and how people in that situation needed support. He then went on to reveal that he too had suffered from depression for many years but this was the day he finally stopped hiding from it. *"I'm not ashamed of my problems, they are part of who I am and don't affect my ability to do my job or to be a good friend or partner."*

Fortunately the treatment I was having did the job and my condition was never as severe as any of those guys'. I eventually stopped taking the tablets through choice, and that's when I discovered that for three months I had been tricked into taking half the prescribed amount! No doubt it was beneficial in the long run and it just shows that the placebo effect does work. Touch wood, pray to God, I'm fine now fortunately.

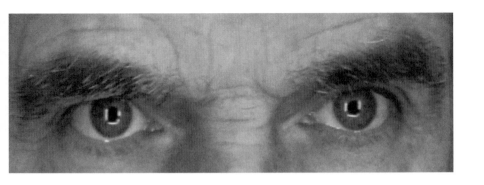

"You can close your eyes to the things you dont want to see, but you cannot close your heart to the things you do not want to feel."

BUST UPS AND FALL-OUTS

NOW as you've probably gathered, either by listening to me on the radio or by reading the first few chapters in this book, I'm opinionated and proud. It's part of who I am and who I always have been. So it won't surprise you to learn than I've had a few bust-ups and fall-outs over the years. Some were my doing, some weren't.

I spent four years playing for Bruce Rioch at Middlesbrough and we were at loggerheads for pretty much all of that time! I recall the build-up to Christmas 1988, we were on course for our second successive promotion, which of course we went on to achieve via the play-offs and I'd scored 17 league and cup goals at that point so I was feeling happy with my contribution. And rightly so, I thought. So when I received a phone call from the club secretary to say that Bruce wanted to see me, I went in with a swagger. I thought "Hey, I'm doing well, he must want to offer me a new contract. Why else would the manager want to see me?" I went up the stairs to his office at Ayresome Park, knocked on the door and took a seat as I waited for him to hand me what I'd expected would be a new contract. But instead he produced two pieces of paper and turned them round so I could see what he'd written on them. He looked at me and said "When you can do them, you'll be a good player". I'd gone in with a swagger but I came out with my head on the floor – I couldn't believe it! When I look at what Bruce wrote now – because I've kept the list – I wonder what on earth Steve McClaren would have said to Michael Ricketts when he called him into his office! The list read:

1. Determination. Running with or without the ball

2. Competing for possession.

3. In the air.

4. To win (with Maradona in brackets).

5. Teamwork. 1 Needs for team.
   2 Needs for self. 3 Passing.
   4 Appreciation. 5 Know-how in general.

6. Creating for others

7. Creating for self.

8. Involvement.

9. Total concentration.

10. Anticipation.

11. Being strong in possession.

12. Don't get knocked off the ball easily.

13 Pass when others want the ball not when you want to release it.

14. Showing for the ball to feet around the edge of the box.

15. Being prepared to work the channels.

16. Being prepared to work with your fellow striker.

17. Heading.

18. Challenging.

19. Strength.

20. Appreciating others in general

I was never a big-time Charlie no matter how many goals I'd scored but Bruce obviously saw something in my make-up that made him want to bring me down a peg or two.

Earlier on that season we went to Plymouth for a league match, which we won 1-0. I was shifted from the centre to play outside left, despite the goals I'd been scoring, and Home Park was never one of my favourite hunting grounds to start with. The majority of players in the team were right-footed so all the play was on the right and I hardly got a kick all game. After the final whistle Bruce was standing in the doorway of the dressing room and as everyone walked past him he was full of compliments to them all... except for me that was. He didn't say a word to me until everyone was in and he slammed the door, turned to me and said "You're a f***ing disgrace." He told me I'd been so poor that I owed my team-mates an apology and he really let rip. I know I'd had a bad game but even though I thought he was being over the top, I took the criticism.

The following week we were at home to Barnsley and when the team sheet was pinned up all the names from one to 11 plus the two subs were listed.... except for No 7 where I'd expected my name to be. It was left completely blank. There was, however, a note at the bottom of the sheet which read "If No 7 wishes to perform today, he can fill the vacant space." I thought what a bastard! I went to the toilet and by the time I came back someone had written Joe Hunt, the kit man's name, in the blank space and all the lads were having a good laugh about it. But that was Bruce's way, I played and I scored in a 2-0 win.

Another time a couple of seasons later after we'd been relegated back to Division Two we played Portsmouth again I was on the left wing which I wasn't happy about. We took a 1-0 lead into the half-time break thanks to Paul Kerr's goal but I was so peed off at being stuck out on the left that when Bruce started praising the lads I just went off on one. I just blew up and said "Listen, I'm on the left wing and not involved at all. You could get a dummy to play there – I'm not playing any more." And I meant it! I really had no intention of going out for the second half and I started chucking my boots off, then my socks, then my shorts. I'd really lost it and I yelled at Bruce "There must be a slant on the pitch because all the balls are going to the right." Bruce had gone for a few of the players in the past and at that point he started making a bee-line for me so I stood up on the bench and shouted at him to get away from me. Bruce stormed out of the dressing room, slamming the door on the way, so his assistant, Colin Todd, turned to my team-mate Mark Proctor and told him "Get him ready. Get his gear on." I still had no intention of doing it myself so there I was, a grown man of 28, in a total strop, with Proc getting me dressed and tying my bootlaces. So thanks to Toddy and Proc I did make it onto the pitch after all and after about 15 or 20 minutes with the score still at 1-0 to us Bruce instructed me to move from the left to the middle. Sure enough I scored and I very quickly made my feelings known to the bench – it wasn't quite a two-fingered salute, more a get it up you! After the game Bruce shook my hand, said "well done" and that was the end of it. He never held grudges which isn't always the case with managers because I've played under some who hold it against you forever if you do or say something they don't like.

I also remember Bruce hammering Gary Pallister after a cup game against a lower division team. He was really laying into him, telling him his head was in the clouds and then he said "I'll tell you what, if you're that big – me and you outside for a fight!" I don't think Bruce would really have rolled his sleeves up and had a punch-up with him, I just think it was the adrenaline pumping. But Bruce was like that.

On another trip away with Boro we stayed in the Thistle Hotel at Potters Bar in Hertfordshire the night before a game at Arsenal. At night the lads started getting a bit restless and before you knew it we were putting tea or sugar in each other's beds or turning the beds upside down. It wasn't quite Rolling Stones stuff, there were no TVs flying out of the window or anything, but there was a good deal of mischief going on and word got out so it ended up making the papers. Bruce Rioch was furious and not for the first time I received a phone call from the secretary to say that Bruce wanted to see me. I arrived mid-afternoon and there were already about ten of the lads waiting – some had been at the ground since nine o'clock in the morning but nothing was going to happen until every one of us was in. Bruce demanded to know who was guilty of making a mess at the hotel and I held my hand up and so did Gary Pallister, who couldn't really deny it because we were room-mates. One or two others didn't come clean, which disappointed me because Pally and I were the only ones fined and the following week Bruce dropped me from the next match against Nottingham Forest. I'd played 136 consecutive matches I travelled and ended up on the bench at the City Ground.

One of the craziest things I got hauled over the coals for was for laughing too much. Honestly. It was during pre-season and in the breaks in between sessions I'd have a laugh and a joke with the lads. But I was always at the front when we were on the training pitch and I always gave it my all so to get dragged into the first team coach's office and be told I was laughing too much was a joke! I told the coach that in no uncertain terms and for the rest of the day captain Tony Mowbray was asked to accompany me. I've no idea why.

When I was at Port Vale we went to play in the Isle of Man Trophy, a pre-season tournament featuring a number of Football League clubs. We made a solid start to the tournament and after a win over Wrexham the manager, John Rudge, told us we could go for a night out as a reward. Unfortunately our next match ended in a heavy defeat. We were absolute garbage so Rudge told the lads they would be no more drinking and that everyone had to be back in their rooms by ten o'clock that night. We all duly arrived back at the hotel in good time for him to tick us off as we went to bed but my team-mate Peter Billing and I had a conversation about going out anyway. There was a back entrance to the hotel and a nightclub not so far away, and we were pretty sure we could sneak out and get back in undetected. We talked to some of the other lads and they thought it was a great idea too. Within an hour the nightclub was full up with lads from the team. I don't drink but the rest of the lads had a few and it was a great night. The following morning when we got up and went to training, John seemed totally oblivious to what had gone on the night before. He had us all sit down in a horseshoe shape with the sun behind us to deliver his team talk, he didn't seem to be any the wiser and we all began to think "We've got away with this." He started talking about our last game and how disappointed he was when suddenly, out of the blue, he pointed to me and said "Were you out last night?" We'd been caught out! If the game was up there was no point in trying to deny it so I decided to be honest and be big enough to put my hand up and admit what I'd done. I had no idea who was behind me but all I could hear were flat denials as Rudgey asked other players if they'd been out as well! I thought I was going to be the only one admitting to it but all of a sudden someone said "Yeah, I was there," followed by someone else and someone else. Almost everyone admitted what they'd done and we all took our fines on the chin. The only one who didn't put his hand up was Ray Walker, the captain. He was thick as thieves with the manager and I didn't like him anyway so I made sure the gaffer found out he had been with us, despite what he'd been saying.

One of the centre-halves at Port Vale while I was there was Peter Swan, who was 6ft 2ins and built like a brick shithouse, but unusually placid with it. We had a behind closed doors game one day with the first team playing the reserves, and he was with the stiffs. Being the centre forward, I was up against him along with Martin Foyle. I went by him and scored, then slipped past him again later in the game but this time he tripped me and conceded a penalty, which I tucked away. As we walked back to our own half after the spot kick Martin Foyle came up to me and said "Next time you try and do that to him, he'll have you." Sure as anything, the next time I was on the ball and about to go past him, he wiped me out. I jumped up and looked at him – at an angle because he was massive and I was 5ft 11in – and said "Just because you're a big bloke you think everyone's scared of you, you f***ing prick!" John Rudge, the manager, was straight over trying to calm things down and I assumed that because the gaffer was getting involved, that would be the end of it. Wrong! I looked over to Rudgey who was within touching distance on my right by then. Then as I turned round to Swanny, the big guy punched me full on it the face. His hands were like shovels and he hit me with such a bang it was unbelievable. I didn't go down, but I could see the birds in front of my eyes and I had concussion for about two weeks. I just looked at him and spat "You're going to get f***ing kneecapped." We finished the match without further incident and when we were in the changing rooms at the stadium, Swanny came over and was all apologetic. I knew he was frustrated at not being in the first team because I'd been in that situation myself but I told him if it was anyone he should be punching it was the manager because he was the one who was keeping him out of the side, not me. That was the end of it after that and we never crossed swords again. Mind you, with my Irish connections, I think he was slightly worried about what my intentions were when I said he was going to get kneecapped! It was just a figure of speech in the heat of the moment though, and in reality he had nothing to fear. I wasn't really going to have him kneecapped!

Training ground bust-ups happen, though. I've seen a few and I've had a few. Stephen Pears and I had one at Hutton Road when we were at Boro. The ball came into the box, I went for it and so did he and we clashed. He threw a handbag and I threw a handbag and unfortunately for us the Tyne Tees TV cameras were there filming us that day for a feature on the local news. As quick as a flash Bruce Rioch was over shouting "Get the cameras off!" Once again that was over and done with as quickly as it started. Incidents like that clear the air and usually you're best mates afterwards. It all happens in the heat of the moment when the adrenaline is pumping and I've never been involved in anything like that which has ever led to any long-term grudges being held.

Being a well-known face in the community, you do sometimes get people trying to wind you up in nightclubs and places like that. I don't drink and I never have but I went to the Tall Trees in Yarm for a night out every weekend for years. I'd be there on a Friday night when I did the matchday commentary, sometimes until the early hours of the morning. It was no problem – there was no danger of having a hangover the next day and if we were away, Ali Brownlee always drove so

I could have a kip in the car if I was feeling tired.

One night I was in there someone came up to me and started having a pop – I can't remember what it was about now but it was to do with football. I said something back to try and diffuse the situation and walked away but the guy followed me and had another jibe. I wasn't going to get involved so I asked the bouncers, who I'd got to know through being a regular there, if they could take him off and calm him down. They were happy to come to my aid and when they took the guy outside they found he was carrying a knife. You can only wonder what would have happened if the situation had escalated.

Then there was the time I was talking to a couple of girls who were sat on stools near the bar when this guy, who was clearly worse for wear, approached us. "Excuse me," he mumbled, brushed past the two lasses, looked at me then hit me full on out of the blue. Once again I called the bouncers over but this time the police came too because I'd been assaulted. His mate who was with him was really apologetic and kept telling me the guy didn't realise it was me and that he'd had a few too many drinks, but that was no excuse for punching someone for no reason, especially when the guy he'd hit was sat on a stool. The bloke was a coward, simple as that. Because the boys in blue were called I found out the guy's name and I also discovered he was a season ticket holder at the Riverside. Boro were at home the following day so I arrived at the ground early and found out where his seat was. My da, who was down visiting at the time, was pretty handy as I've mentioned before and he was all for finding him and sorting him out, but I told him to leave it because he wasn't worth it. I don't know whether he was sleeping off his hangover or sitting at home feeling remorseful but he never turned up for the match anyway that day. The police had visited me before the match to talk to me about the incident and to take pictures of my face, although I don't bruise easily so there wasn't much evidence I'd been punched. I was all for going through the courts to see him punished but then I heard his wife was pregnant and due to give birth quite soon. His family didn't need a court appearance and criminal record to deal with at a time like that so I dropped the charges.

That guy obviously didn't know who I was, but I suppose some people just think you're fair game if they've had a few drinks and see you out and about. I was at The Mall in Stockton one night after I'd scored a hat-trick for Boro when some guy came over to me and started verbally abusing me and telling me I was crap. Of all the nights to criticise me! I'd just scored a hat-trick but that still wasn't good enough! It just goes to show that you can't please some people, but I would say that these are only isolated incidents. I'd often be out three or four times a week sometimes and unsavoury incidents were few and far between. I like a bit of banter, don't get me wrong. You just get one or two absolute arseholes who just want to embarrass you in front of people.

On another occasion my then wife, had gone into Middlesbrough for a drink. I drove into town to pick her up at around 11 o'clock, which was around about the time the revellers who were a bit worse for wear were spilling out onto the streets deciding which nightclub to head off to so they could carry on drinking. My missus jumped into the car next to me and I was about to drive off but there were three guys stood in front of the car having a chat. I waited a while but when they didn't move, I asked them politely if they'd shift out of the way, but what I got in return was a volley of abuse and V signs. F*** you lads! If being nice wasn't going to work, I'd have to find a Plan B. So I reversed slightly, then stuck the car in first gear and bang! I drove into them and knocked the bastards up in the air. I looked in my mirror to check they were OK and one of them must have had matches in his pocket because his trousers were on fire, but apart from that they seemed fine. They looked very shocked though, so I bet they never did that again.

We always had a loyal audience on the Legends with some listeners calling in regularly during our time on air. Among them was a Boro fan called Frank who used to ring in every couple of weeks. He was very critical and opinionated and was always a good caller, I liked his style so we always got along well. Apart from one night, that is. We'd all been asked to tell funny stories away from football and I recounted the time my big, 30-stone mate popped round to visit me. While I was out walking my dogs I collected some rabbit droppings, then when I got home I covered them in chocolate and put them in a dish on the table. It was a hot, summer day and when my mate strolled in, his eyes were instantly drawn to what he thought was a big pile of tasty chocolates. Sure enough he asked if he could have some and I said "Go ahead big man." There he was shoving them in his gob and chewing them and that point I was convinced the game was up but instead, he just swallowed and asked if he could have some more! I told this story on air and shortly afterwards Frank phoned up and he wasn't happy. "I just want to say you're out of order regarding that story," he told me. "It was horrible, disgusting, vulgar and totally unacceptable. That story should not have been aired." He went on and on and even went as far as saying I should be taken off air! I was flabbergasted. "Have you not got any mates?" I asked him. "Have you never had a bit of horseplay?" Don't forget I'm a Celebrity Get Me Out Of Here is a prime time TV show and they eat all sorts of stuff on that. Cockroaches, kangaroo testicles, pig brains, roasted spider... it all gets served up on that show and it's on TV so you can actually see people eating it. Frank was still having none of it so I offered to apologise but he fumed "I don't want your apology." So I started winding him up and asked him if he'd prefer to eat rabbit poo or a kangaroo's testicle but he said he didn't want to eat either and called me an idiot. "You've not heard the end of this," he warned me, "I'm taking this further. You don't know who you're dealing with." I told him if he wanted me sacked he should go for it but I was fuming. I'd been doing this gig for 12 or 13 years and I knew how to keep my cool but this time it had really got under my skin, especially when he told me he wanted to see me sacked. I've no idea if he did take it further, although I'm sure I'd have heard about it if he did, but three weeks later Frank was on the phone again. The lad who worked in the studio when we were on air came running in to tell me who was calling, which is something he never normally did, but I was happy enough to talk to him. I greeted him with "Hello Frank, I'm still here," and that was it – the conversation continued as if nothing had happened. We talked about whatever was happening at Boro at the time and he went on calling as regularly as before. It was totally bizarre.

Another topic that had Frank rattled was when, on the spur of the moment, I decided to spark an offbeat debate. "Come on Malcolm," I said, "Margaret Thatcher or Myra Hindley?" Being a true blue Tory, Malcolm had no hesitation in choosing Maggie, saying what a wonderful woman she was and soon we had a huge political debate on our hands. Colin Emerson e-mailed in to say "Margaret Thatcher is evil personified – we will have a massive party when the bastard dies." Frank weighed in with "Pathetic comments about Thatcher.

Why don't you Labour supporters realise it was your pathetic party that just about brought the country to its knees? Get your head out of the sand!" I was reading these out and Colin hit straight back "You don't real- ise, Frank, how her policies crippled the North-East. You're probably forgetting your family's roots. A man who forgets where he came from is a sad character in my eyes." So it went on, with other listeners getting involved – it must have been a cracking show to listen to with so many people on either side of the political fence venting their spleen. Bernie Lowe e-mailed in to say "See what you've started Bernie? Politics and foot- ball discussions, no matter what party you support, we were changing from an industrial age to a technologi- cal age so something had to give and it just happened to happen in Thatcher's reign." What a backlash to an off the cuff comment! As it happens Frank still phones me to this day on CVFM.

The post-match radio phone-in that Ali and I did used to go on long after the fans had left the ground and we were taking calls as usual after Boro's FA Cup match against Nuneaton Borough when at around 10 o'clock Mark Schwarzer came out onto the pitch with Paul Barron, the goalkeeping coach, to do a training routine. He'd been left out of the team in favour of Brad Jones because the match was against a lower league club but he was nevertheless a wee bit peeved at being rested, and you can't blame him because he was a great keeper. Ali and I were at the back of the stand near another radio guy from Nuneaton but apart form Schwarzer and Barron there was nobody else about in the stadium. When they'd finished on the pitch they started heading towards the tunnel and Schwarzer had four or five balls in his hands. He put them down and then started booting the balls up towards us! It wasn't Ali he was aiming for because they were quite pally, but fortunately he was a bad shot and the balls nestled all over the stand instead of reaching us but I was talking to a caller at the time so I couldn't respond. Schwarzer disappeared down the tunnel straight away but Barron was walking about 20 yards behind him – he started saying something but I couldn't hear him because I had my headphones on. So when we hit the break I took my headphones off and asked him what he wanted. "Give us the balls back, will you," he replied. You what? No way was I going round collecting balls that had been booted at us while we were on air! I said "Do you think I'm the ball boy? You can f*** right off!" I've no idea who did come to collect them, but needless to say it wasn't me. The following Saturday I saw Barron before the game so I decided to have a word with him about the incident. I told him that if I'd done what Schwarzer had when Bruce Rioch was in charge, he'd have booted my arse and told me to go up and get them myself. "Why didn't you do that," I asked him. But, and this sums the modern game up for me, he said "With the money they're on these days, how can you tell them?"

Unsettled Slaven set for Rioch showdown

By RAY ROBERTSON

MIDDLESBROUGH striker Bernie Slaven will have talks this week with manager Bruce Rioch over his future.

The Boro's leading scorer is unsettled over being relegated to the role of substitute for the last two games.

Slaven was previously an ever-present for three seasons following a £25,000 move from Albion Rovers.

Rioch refused to comment on a report that Slaven has been fined, along with Gary Pallister and Gary Hamilton.

It is believed disciplinary action was taken over a hotel incident on a recent London trip.

Rioch said: "I don't discuss internal ...."

The Boro boss has denied Manchester United have made a £900,000 bid for midfield player Mark ......

Bernie Slaven

"Brennan has settled in well at Ayresome Park following his summer move from Ipswich.

"Mark has the ability to score and create goals.

"Brennan has responded with two goals against Nottingham Forest and Aston Villa.

"I still think Brennan can improve. He is a talented player."

Rioch was thrilled over his team's fightback against Aston Villa.

"Even when we conceded two quick goals, I thought we could get back into the game with a quick goal.

"The players showed exceptional character in their fightback. It was disappointing not to collect three points but I think we would have settled for a draw at seven minutes past three."

England Under-21 international winger Stuart Ripley suffered a first-half hamstring injury.

Ripley could miss the Simod Cup tie against Oldham Athletic on Wednesday night, and the First Division match against Charlton on Saturday.

Middlesbrough are happy with a home FA Cup tie against Grimsby Town.

One of many paper cuttings

IT'S A FUNNY OLD GAME

SEE what I mean about a rollercoster? But for every down there has been an up and I've got plenty of funny stories to tell from my life as a footballer and a broadcaster.

Footballers are known to like playing practical jokes on each other and there's always some sort of horseplay going on. It still happens now. You'll come into the dressing room to find your shoes nailed to the floor, the bottom of your tie chopped off or Ralgex sprayed on your underpants so that when you put them on your balls sting like you wouldn't believe. Sometimes someone would hide your gear too. I always wore the No 7 shirt and I'd often have to go looking for it because one of my mischievous teammates had hidden it.

At the start of the 1989/90 season Middlesbrough signed a blond midfielder called Trevor Putney from Norwich City, and he was a real character. He was always hammering his team-mates and I remember being out training at Ayresome Park one cold, rainy day. We were doing a stretch at the Holgate End and as I was talking to one of the lads on my right I started feeling this warm sensation on my left. I thought for a moment I'd pulled my hamstring but when I turned round there was Putney peeing on my leg!

Trevor missed Boro's appearance against Chelsea in the 1990 Zenith Data Systems Cup final at Wembley through injury but, despite being on crutches, he travelled south and stayed overnight with the team in our hotel. I was rooming with Mark Proctor who had a boot deal with one of the sportswear companies and he was phoning round the players and inviting them to come and collect their boots for the big game. After they were all distributed there was an aggressive knock on our door and when Proc opened it, in staggered Putters. He'd quite clearly been on the drink and bawled "Where's my f***ing boots Proctor?" As Proc tried to give him an explanation, Putters started knocking stuff all over our hotel room with one of his crutches. I can't remember him apologising the following morning, either!

On the subject of the Zenith Data Systems Cup, when we reached the semi-finals a businessman called Henry Moszkowicz went public and promised the players £1,000 a man if we achieved our goal of getting Boro to Wembley for the first time in the club's history. Moszkowicz was a board member and part of the consortium that stopped the club from going under in 1986, but we never did receive the money, despite our historic achievement. By all accounts he wasn't allowed to do it but he could have bought us a gift, like a watch or something, but we received neither.

I'm no different to the rest of the lads in that I've played my share of practical jokes. I gave as good as I got though and on one occasion I filled Gary Gill's bag with horse dung and left it. We'd been away for a few days with the club but I managed to get hold of the key to his hotel room, put the manure in his bag and then some of his gear over the top so he couldn't see what I'd done. It started to really stink after a couple of days away. During the 1991/92 season I suffered a bucket handle tear to the cartilage in my knee and I needed an operation to have it removed. At the time I was good friends with Gary Parkinson and Mark Proctor and I seized the opportunity to have them on. After I'd had the operation I asked Tommy Johnson, the physio, to get me a specimen bottle and a piece of Tubigrip, which is a skin-coloured bandage you use to dress a corn or a bunion. I cut the Tubigrip into the shape of a bucket handle and dropped it into the specimen bottle which I filled with water and when Parky came in to ask me how the operation went I said to him "Look at this, it's what they took out." I showed him the Tubigrip in the specimen bottle and it looked quite convincing – in fact so convincing that he didn't know any different until a couple of years ago when I went to visit him and came clean.

Another occasion I look back and laugh about involved Mick Saxby who was a fringe player at Middlesbrough. Mick looked like a porn star with his mop of curly hair and thick moustache, and he was always injured. In fact I don't think I ever saw him play because he was always having treatment for something or another. On this particular day I was injured too so Steve Smelt, the physio, gave me a list of things to do in the gym and off I went to do them. Saxby, though, was nowhere to be seen. When I'd finished I headed down to the snooker room they had at Ayresome Park – low and behold, there was Saxby at the table, cue in hand. I'm not an especially good snooker player but I took up his offer of a game. All the time we were playing I couldn't help thinking that I was drenched in sweat after my work-out while Saxby, who was nowhere to be seen in the gym, was dry as a bone. The fact he'd been skiving off was obviously on his mind too because he kept checking his watch as we were playing. Eventually he got a glass of water, splashed it all over his hair, face and shirt and suddenly you couldn't tell who had been to the gym and who hadn't!

On the subject of porn stars… It reminds me of the regular routine Pally, Don O'Riordan and I used to have on the occasions we were in for morning and afternoon training sessions during pre-season. I lived in Westbourne Road in the middle of town at the time, so we'd pick up a Slush Puppy and a sausage roll, take it back to my house and watch a porno film until it was time to go back to training! We'd be running with three legs when the session started. I'm not sure what the modern players would make of that but, then again, maybe they do the same!

Just before my first Christmas on Teesside I was delighted to learn that all the players would be given a free turkey and a bottle of wine from the club. Now I don't drink so the wine wasn't much use to me although it would be handy to have in for guests, but the turkey was a different matter. I couldn't wait to get my hands on that, so after being told where to go to collect it, I dashed down first to make sure I could pick up the biggest turkey I could find. Sure enough I found a real whopper. I couldn't wait to tuck into that on Christmas Day, but when I got it home I discovered it wouldn't fit in the oven!

Usually if you've got a tasty cream cake or something similar to tuck in to, one of the boys would pretend it's off and tell you to smell it... then shove it into your nose when you did. An old routine but it never failed. I decided to do something similar when we were staying in a hotel with Port Vale down at Dartmoor. I was sitting next to the coach driver who was looking particularly smart in his suit and tie and we were having a good chat about this, that and the other, when I decided to play the old joke on him. Our dinner looked lovely – roast chicken, potatoes, vegetables and gravy – but I said to him "Smell this will you?" I'd only intended to dab the mashed potatoes lightly on his nose but as I tipped the plate, the whole dinner slid down onto his suit! I was so embarrassed but the lads thought it was hilarious and they were creased up laughing. The driver wasn't too happy but I got away with it.

John Hendrie soon found out about our sense of humour at Middlesbrough. When he first arrived at the club from Leeds in 1990 I told the lads we should get him with the spoons – the idea being that the two of us kneel down facing each other, each with a big spoon in our mouth. One of us then turns round and the other, using the power in his jaw, has to whack the other one on the back of his head with a spoon. Obviously it's not that easy to do but when it was my turn I had Stuart Ripley behind Hendie with a spoon in his hand to give poor John a big whack! It happened about six or seven times before he found out what was going on.

As I've mentioned before, we were always up for a good night out and I was no different even though I'm teetotal. One night we were at the Tall Trees, our regular haunt, and Gary Pallister had put a few drinks away so I suggested he stayed over at my place. Karen and I only just moved in and we were a bit upside down and because we were still in the process of moving our furniture in, so we only had one bed. Karen, was back up in Glasgow at the time so I told Pally he could take the right-hand side and, I'd take the left and we'd put some cushions down the middle. I'd roomed with Pally for years so neither of us had a problem with that – it was a practical solution to the situation. We didn't have training the next morning so there was no rush to get up, but the curtains were open and when I woke up, there was the window cleaner, cleaning the window! I've no idea what he thought of seeing two Boro players in bed together! Thank God there were no mobile phones with cameras back then. Can you imagine the reaction if he'd taken a quick snap and taken it to the papers? Pally's a good mate but we're not that close!

One memory I have from my time with the Republic of Ireland team was the build-up to our match against England in a European Championship qualifier at Wembley Stadium in March 1991. We'd stayed down in London and our final training session consisted of a warm-up, a five-a-side game before Jack Charlton put Tony Cascarino and Niall Quinn in goal, told the rest of the lads to grab a ball each. Packie Bonner and Gerry Peyton were the two goalkeepers in the squad but Big Jack had two centre-forwards in goal while the rest of us had to try and score a goal by chipping them. I'd never known anything like it! Cascarino and Quinny weren't allowed to handle the ball, only head it away, and that was our final training session before a massive match at Wembley. As it turned out we held England to a 1-1 draw so it shows it doesn't matter what you do in training, it's what you do on matchday that counts.

I spent three years with Ireland and there were some great lads in the squad, and one of them was Paul McGrath. He was a lovely lad and a great player but he liked a drink. The team always met in the Airport Hotel in Dublin and one Sunday afternoon we assembled there ahead of our next game as usual. We arrived in the afternoon, went to our rooms to get ourselves sorted, then arranged to meet in the foyer that evening to go and get something to eat. We all congregated ready to go out, except for Paul who was nowhere to be seen, so we went off to have our meal without him. After we'd eaten we were all back in the foyer when in came Paul – absolutely steaming drunk and being held up by two lads.

The game wasn't until the Wednesday but there was no way Big Jack or the management team wanted a repeat of that so they emptied the mini-bar in his room and the physio, a guy called Mick Byrne, slept in the aisle outside the door of Paul's room that night so he couldn't sneak out for a drink. Come the Wednesday I was only the 17th man in a 17-man squad because I'd only played one international game. Only 16 players would be officially stripped for action so I didn't bother taking my boots because I knew I wasn't going to be involved. We arrived at Lansdowne Road nice and early for the game and there were already about 20,000 fans there as we walked out onto the pitch… and they were all singing "Ooh ahh Paul McGrath." If only they knew what had been going on all week. He was a hero to the supporters though and they were all looking forward to seeing him play. When we returned to the dressing room Big Jack started to read out the team: "Bonner, Staunton, Morris, McCarthy…" But as he was reading out the name "McGrath", he lifted his head only to discover the fans' favourite defender had disappeared. Fuming, he instantly looked at me and barked "Get stripped." Suddenly I was in the 16-man matchday squad but I didn't have my boots! Noel King was the youth team coach at the time and he was happy enough to lend me his – the trouble was he was a size seven-and-a-half and I was a nine! There was no other option though, and I sat on the bench for the whole game hoping I wouldn't get on because I couldn't feel my toes, the boots were so tight. Needless to say I didn't get on – I think Jack must have watched me warm up.

The Airport Hotel was a regular stopping place for the Republic team and on another visit there I'd eaten a few too many Dublin Bay prawns and I started to feel a bit sick. The room I was in was hot and stuffy and, for safety reasons, you couldn't open the windows very wide so there wasn't a lot of ventilation. I was rooming with Alan McLoughlin, the Swindon lad, and we were playing the next day so I didn't want to disturb him. It was about half past 12 or one o'clock in the morning, so I ventured out of the room to try and get some fresh air. As I approached the foyer I spotted Big Jack and Maurice Setters, his No 2, sitting there having a drink. I really didn't want them to see me out of my room at that time of night, even though I had a perfectly valid reason, so I cut through some double doors and found myself in the courtyard with a big, 12-foot wall around it. The beer kegs for the bar were stacked up next to the wall so there was only one thing for it – climb up them and jump over the wall. I'm from Glasgow, you think of things like that. I knew there was grass and some trees on the other side, and that's exactly where I need-ed to be to breathe in some fresh air. So over I went and there I was, walking through the woods with my Ireland trackie on tak-ing nice, deep breaths but within five minutes I was surrounded by officers of the Garda demanding to know who I was and what I was doing scaling a wall. "Get your hands up," they barked at me as the shone a light in my face, so I did as I was told and did my best to convince them that, despite my Scottish accent, I was a member of the Republic of Ireland football team. Eventually they believed me, thankfully, although I still had to go back in through the front entrance and get past Jack without him seeing me. I'm pleased to say I managed that too.

Big Jack was a proud Englishman, and a World Cup winner too, but he loved Ireland and the Irish loved him. One of the ways he used to get us fired up for matches was to play a compilation tape of songs he'd had made on the team bus. We'd get to within 20 minutes or so of the ground and he'd make sure it was on. There were songs such as Under Pressure, Molly Malone, some of the famous traditional Irish songs… and a few rebel songs too. These songs would be blaring out through the speakers to get the players charged up as is if they were going into battle. One of the songs he used to play was Sean South of Garryowen, and Jack used to sing along to it – although he didn't really know the ins and outs of what it was about. The song is actually about killing Englishmen and Sean South was an IRA member who died in a raid on an RUC barracks in County Fermanagh! Here are the words:

Sad are the homes round Garryowen
Since they lost their joy and pride
And the banshee cry links every vale
Around the Shannon side that city of the ancient walls
the broken treaty stone, undying fame surrounds your name, Sean
South from Garryowen

T'was on a dreary New Year's Eve
As the shades of night came down
A lorry load of volunteers approached the border town
There were men from Dublin and from Cork, Fermanagh and

Tyrone

And the leader was a Limerick man - Sean South from Garryowen

As they moved along the street up to the barracks door

They scorned the danger they might face

Their fate that lay in store

They were fighting for old Ireland to claim their very own

And the foremost of that gallant band

Was South from Garryowen

But the sergeant spied their daring plan

He spied them through the door

The Sten guns and the rifles a hail of death did pour

And when that awful night had passed

Two men lay cold a stone

There was one from near the border and one from Garryowen

No more will he hear the seagull's cry

Over the murmuring Shannon tide

For he fell beneath a Northern sky brave Hanlon by his side

They have gone to join that gallant band

Of Plunkett, Pearse and Tone

A martyr for old Ireland

Sean South from Garryowen

Songwriters: S COSTELLO.Lyrics © ESSEX MUSIC INC
C/O THE RICHMOND ORGANIZATION

Jack was asked on one occasion how he got the team focussed and pumped up for a big game and he replied "We play Sean South." Well as you can imagine, it ended up all over the papers, MPs were going mad about it – but he really didn't know what the song was about. Funnily enough though, he never played it again after that.

You also get to hear a lot of tales when you're a player, and one time when I was rooming with Terry Phelan during a Republic of Ireland away game I was asking him about Wimbledon and their antics over the years. The Dons were known as the Crazy Gang, of course, and were always making the news for something or another, but the story Terry told me which stuck in my mind was when his manager at the time called him in the office and accused him of being disruptive and arrogant. He then apparently went on to say "Do you know your problem, Terry? You don't know if you're black or white!" Terry went home and repeated that to his father, who wanted to march straight to the stadium and kill his son's boss!

I've had plenty of laughs during my radio career too. Back in December 1998 after Boro had beaten West Ham 1-0 at the Riverside, we were doing the phone-in as usual when, near the end of the show, my sidekick Ali Brownlee turned to me and said "Next week Bernard, we go to Old Trafford, the Theatre of Dreams, to take on Manchester United. How far would you go if we actually beat them?" I quizzed him on when Boro had last won there. "Sixty-eight years ago," he replied.

There is a saying in Middlesbrough that if there's no way on earth you can imagine a certain situation or event happening, you'd show your arse in the window of Binns, the local department store, if it did. United were on their way to a remarkable treble that season, and there was no way I could see Boro breaking that long winless streak this time. So without hesitation I told Ali "I will show my arse in Binns window if it comes off." Ali was leaving nothing to chance and promised me he would go and have a word with the department store manager first thing on Monday morning. And later that day he phoned me to confirm that the manager had reluctantly agreed. Ali had sold it on good PR for the store, loads of exposure – if you'll pardon the pun - and assured him that there was only a very slim chance of it coming off.

The following week I was perched on my seat in the press box at Old Trafford and we were winning 2-0! Remembering what I'd vowed on air to do, the Boro fans away to my right were singing "Bernie, Bernie, show us your arse." Astonishingly it got even better for Boro as Brian Deane added to goals from Hamilton Ricard and Dean Gordon to make it 3-0. I had half a bum cheek out by then! United pulled one back through Nicky

Butt and then Paul Scholes made it 3-2 – if I'm being honest, I was thinking "Come on United, score a third and get me off the hook, a draw is still a good result." With only a few minutes to go a long ball over the top of Boro's defence left former Newcastle United striker Andy Cole one-on-one with Mark Schwarzer. I was thinking "Go on, put it in!" But I should have known better -typical Newcastle striker, he missed it. The full-time whistle went and the 5,000 travelling Boro supporters were once again chanting "Bernie, Bernie, show us your arse," only this time louder. Within 15 minutes I was surrounded by the national media, wanting to know on what the chanting was all about.

The following morning, despite my team's amazing achievement in winning away to a side that was on its way to winning the Premiership, FA Cup and Champions League and putting an end to that 68-year Old Trafford hoodoo, all the headlines belonged to me. "Bernie gets the bum's rush" and things like that. For me that sums up the media. In their defence it was December and all the hacks were looking for a feelgood story, something different to the norm.

True to my word, on the Monday morning I arrived at the office of the Binns manager, which was on the third floor of the store. He was nervously dabbing his brow and looking at Ali saying

"I don't know why I ever agreed to this, you told me it wasn't likely to happen." Ali wasn't flustered at all though, and told him, "Don't worry the publicity for you will be fantastic." He was right. There was a knock on the door it was the Daily Mail, then came the Express, the Times, Gazette, Northern Echo, Mirror, Tyne Tees TV, Sky... Within half an hour the room was jam-packed with people from the media. Then came a firm knock on the door - it was PC Plod. In he marched demanding to know "Where is the gentleman that is doing the dirty deed?" Then he turned to me and warned "Can I just remind you that if you don't wear underwear you will be arrested - and can you get a move on."

That was me told, so off I went and I was escorted into the lift by two burly bouncers. I was wearing a white shirt, my kilt and a pair of red knickers, with 2-3 in pen on my cheeks which a young girl had kindly written. As the lift doors opened I saw the ground floor was rammed, it was about ten deep either side. The only way I can describe it was like a boxer going into the ring, only I was going into the window. As I headed to my allotted space people were squeezing my bum cheeks, lifting up my kilt and shouting all sorts of obscenities. When I arrived at my destination the shutters were down, and as I looked at the crowds behind me I assumed everyone must have been in the store. I thought that when the shutters went up there would only be a couple of cameramen outside looking in. How wrong I was! When the shutters lifted there was a huge crowd of 2,000 people waiting for a glimpse of my rear, young kids, grannies, grandads, people up poles on each other's shoulders. It was unbelievable.

The comment of the day came from an old lady at the front. Remember it was Christmas-time and, as I lifted my kilt to reveal my hairless buttocks, the lady shouted "That reminds me, I have to stuff the turkey."

I remember heading out to the Czech Republic in September 2005 for Middlesbrough's historic first ever European away match against Banik Ostrava in the UEFA Cup. We checked into our hotel and the receptionist told us there was a sauna in the basement we could use. That seemed like a good idea so Ali Brownlee, John Hendrie and I all decided to give it a go. Some of the English lads coming the other way told us it might not be such a good idea but they didn't elaborate and we carried on going. But when we arrived at the sauna we found out what they meant because we were the only ones wearing anything! There were men and women everywhere completely starkers – I felt embarrassed for having pants on!

When we were covering the home leg at the Riverside Stadium

one of the assistant referees was a woman called Corinne La-grange from France. I didn't mention it at the time but when Malcolm asked me how the game had gone at the start of the following evening's Legends show, I said "We've waited 128 years for European football to come to Middlesbrough and when it does they give us a woman linesman!" I turned to Gatesy and said "Can you imagine if you're at the pub with your mates and one of them asks where your lass is, and you say 'She's down at the Boro officiating'. They'd all take the p***. She shouldn't be running the line at a European football match, she should be at home look-ing after the kids, taking the dog for a walk, cleaning the house or something like that." I knew there would be some reaction to that and the first caller was a woman who asked to talk to "the male chauvinist pig". I told her I didn't like being called a pig but I took her call and she hammered me. She gave me what for, told me how women were working hard to get that far and was having none of it. At the end she calmed down so I said "Can I ask you one question? Are you married?" She said she wasn't so I ended the conversation with "Well there's a surprise!" These days you wouldn't get away with that, but I don't see why not.

Malcolm Macdonald earned himself a new nickname on another occasion after we had been to the Metro Centre signing books. A lady walked up to us, she didn't buy a book, but she looked at me and said "I don't know who you are." I told her that was okay as I was from Middlesbrough and this was Tyneside so she'd probably never come across me before, then she looked at Micky Horswill and said "I don't know who you are either." But when she looked at Malcom she said "I know who you are though." Malcolm puffed his chest out like a prize pigeon, only to be told "You're Trevor McDonald." Malcolm's chest soon deflated after that.

Signing books was an annual event for us at the Metro and another year when we were there Malcolm made a point of greeting everyone in his poshest voice. "Oh hello there, how are you," he would say before taking what seemed like two days to sign each book in his beautiful handwriting. All the while he was doing this I was trying to think of whose voice his sounded like and eventually it came to me – John Merrick, the Elephant Man. That night on the Legends show I asked Malcolm to tell the listeners how he'd been greeting people that day, which he did, then I threw it open. I asked the listeners to phone in and tell me who I thought he sounded like, with a signed book to the first person who got it right. Julian Clary was one early answer, followed by a few other gay icons before Peter the Boro Fan got it right. The next day we were back at the Metro Centre signing more books when some guy marched over to the table. He pointed to Malcolm and said "You might sound like the Elephant Man," then pointed to Micky and said "You f***ing look like him" and walked away.

We always liked to be topical on the Legends show and sometimes it wasn't just football matters that caught our eye. I remember back in August 2010 we were in the studio and I said to Malcolm "What about the woman who put that cat in a bin?" It was all over the news at the time. For some reason this woman, Mary Bale her name was, picked up a tabby cat and threw it in a wheely bin in Coventry and it was caught on CCTV. There was a massive public outcry at what she did and I'm an animal lover so I said to Malcolm while we were on air "I'd love to have thrown her in a bin!" A few minutes later I received a text saying "I don't know what all the fuss is about – Top Cat's been in a bin for 30 years!" It was a serious matter but that gave us a laugh.

Just before one show I came up with the idea of pretending to play the bagpipes. I spoke to Rodders who drove the show and asked him to find a soundbite of some bagpipes playing and, quick as a shot, he came up with the goods. I usually started the show but I got Malcolm to do it on this occasion and we made the bagpipes sound as if they were in distance and getting closer as though I was approaching the studio. Gatesy announced I was warming up my bagpipes outside and the listeners could hear screeching in the distance before I made my way in to the studio playing Scotland the Brave, or so we made out anyway. Every now and then I would breathe very heavily as if I'd actually been playing and after another Scottish classic we threw it open to the listeners and asked them "What would you like Bernie to play next?" The calls, e-mails and texts flooded in and I received comments like "I didn't know you could play the bagpipes – a man of many talents" and one listener even invited me to play at a wedding! To get away with playing the bagpipes on a football show in England takes some doing! I came clean about two months later.

We were also known to have a laugh at each others' expense. One night a Sunderland fan phoned in to talk to Micky Horswill and because he had quite a high-pitched voice, we assumed he was quite young. Micky took the call and, believing he was talking to a lad of 14 or 15, said "Hello, how old are you, son?" "I'm 45," came the reply! On another occasion Malcom Macdonald was filling in for Bob Moncur who commentated on Newcastle matches in the same way I did the Middlesbrough games. He couldn't make it to this particular game so Malcolm was despatched to St James' Park, leaving me and Gatesy in the studio. Before the game we spoke to him on air about the game, asked him to run through the teams and give us the formations. All was going well until he told us Newcastle were playing a 5-4-3-1 formation! He had them down as playing with 13 men. No wonder they were winning every week.

Being a Newcastle legend Malcolm was despised by the Sunderland fans – they'd have him done away with in as second! One night he made the big mistake of leaving the press box to get a half-time cup of tea at a Sunderland v Newcastle match, even though Gatesy had advised him to stay put, and came back covered in pies that had been thrown at him. On another occasion we were in the studio when someone emailed in to say "Malcolm's boring me, sort him out will you?" So during the break I asked the producer to find me the sound of a gunshot to play. So before the end of the show I read the email and said "OK, I'm going to oblige. Malcolm, take this!" Bang! I played the gunshot sound and told the listeners "Join us again tomorrow for the Two Legends." The following night when we started the show I welcomed our listeners to the Two Legends and Malcolm stayed completely silent. Eventually we made a comment about seeing Malcolm's car pull in to the car park and agreed I must have missed him when I pulled the trigger because there he was arriving at the studio. Some time afterwards we received a letter – just the one – from a guy who wanted me sacked because I'd "shot" Malcolm. I couldn't believe it, especially as the guy didn't have the balls to phone in and say it to my ear. I went off on one when we were next on air and said "Have you never seen a John Wayne film? He shoots everybody!" I can look back and laugh at that now but it's another indication that there's always someone somewhere who wants you sacked for the most trivial of reasons and that does my head in.

Malcolm was at the centre of it again when we were discussing Salvador Cabanas, a Paraguayan player that Sunderland, managed at the time by Steve Bruce, were trying to sign in early 2010. And this time it was Malcolm who had "killed" someone. It emerged one night when we were doing the Legends show that Cabanas had been shot in the head in a Mexico City bar. We didn't know at that time how serious his injuries were, but naturally we wished him well and hoped that Sunderland would still be able to bring him to England. The following night I began as usual by welcoming listeners to the show when suddenly Malcolm cut across and started offering his condolences to the lad's family because he'd sadly passed away as a result of the shooting. That was very commendable but he wasn't dead! In fact he went on to make a comeback after recovering sufficiently from his injuries and he's still alive today! So I was looking across at Malcolm and shaking my head and trying to tell him that I'd heard nothing to suggest he'd died but Malcolm was having none of it. Fortunately Malcolm was able to be convinced he'd been given duff information and he started the following night's show by offering his apologies.

It wasn't the only time Malcolm put his foot in it. In June 2013 we were on air discussing England's dismal performance at the European Under-21 Championships. They'd finished bottom of their group in Israel without a single point, which was even worse than their poor showing in Denmark two years earlier. I made the point that with so many foreign players over here now, the English lads were being squeezed out and not getting any opportunities. Malcolm agreed but unfortunately he could have phrased it better. "The reason we get players from places like Africa," he said, "is because they've got the hunger." Not a good choice of words.

Then there was the time Malcolm said on air that Newcastle United would never wear red shirts. "Never, never, never," he repeated. However a caller rang in to suggest the club actually wore red shirts when they were formed and it was also pointed out that Malcolm himself had worn a red shirt on the day Newcastle were famously beaten by non-league Hereford United in the 1972 FA Cup third round when Ronnie Radford scored a belter. Mind you, that was such an embarrassing result that he probably did his best to forget everything he could about the day!

I can sympathise with Malcom at being pelted with pies because I know what it's like to get a reaction from fans of other teams when you're at a game, although unlike him I didn't end up with my coat covered in meat and potato filling. I'd gone to St James' Park to take in a game with Gary Pallister while he was at Manchester United and I was at Port Vale. Not long into the match a large section of the fans stood up, faced us, and started chanting "Who the f*** are Man Utd?" The chant went on for a while and, as it was coming to an end, one solitary voice yelled "And who the f*** are Port Vale?" Everyone had a good laugh at that, then sat down again and focussed on the game.

Another example of how you have to be careful what you say on air was during Dong Gook Lee's short and not especially successful time at Boro. He was a Korean international signed by Gareth Southgate in January 2007 and, although he was less than prolific in front of goal for the club, it didn't take long for the fans to give him his own song and, one night a regular caller by the name of Colin phoned us on the Legends to give us a rendition. "He shoots, he scores, he eats labradors," chanted Colin as we listened in on the other end of the phone line. I was creased up laughing and asked him to sing it again for us. The following day Jon Kirby, one of the gaffers, called us in and told us we couldn't encourage things like that and in future we should block it right away. I'll be honest, I found it humorous rather than offensive and Malcolm was quick to chip in too. "I've been over there," he piped up, "and they do eat dogs!" If that's what they do and if it's their culture, that's up to them but the next time Colin came on and tried to sing the song, we had to stop him.

We used to get a lot of texts and emails and as a rule I used to read the funny ones and Malcolm would do the boring ones, but because of the busy nature of the show there wasn't always time to look at them before they were read out. One such occasion was early on in Chris Hughton's reign as caretaker manager at

Newcastle following their relegation in 2008. He actually did a good job and led them back in to the Premier League but not everyone was convinced he was the man for the job, among them the guy who texted in to say "Chris Hughton is a worse caretaker than Ian Huntley." It was a busy night, I hadn't seen the text prior to reading it out live on the air and it didn't register. I carried on reading out texts we'd received until we got to the break when Jon Kirby came over to me and told me what I'd done. Ian Huntley, of course, was the school caretaker who murdered two schoolgirls in Soham, but it just didn't click as I was reading out the text. If I'm honest I think I thought Huntley possibly could have been a previous caretaker manager of Newcastle, after all I'm no expert on the history of the club. I'm no fan of sick jokes and there's no way I would have read it out as a way of trying to get a laugh. As soon as we went back on air I apologised. I've always liked to think I'm quick and sharp but on this occasion I boobed massively.

Fortunately occasions like that hardly ever happened although I did require another bit of outside help to point me in the right direction when I was commentating on a game at the Riverside and Jimmy Floyd Hasselbaink scored one of his many goals for the club. This time, though, I knew I needed someone else to help me. After putting the ball in the back of the net, Jimmy ran behind the goal, went up to the fans in the New Holgate

End and started flapping his arms like a wild bird. I was telling the listeners what a great goal it was – superb composure, lovely chip, wonderful finish, but I didn't quite get the celebration. Did anyone know what he was doing? A couple of days later someone told me he'd heard me on the radio and had the answer – it turns out the players had been shown a video of flying geese! As a form of motivation, the squad had all been sat down to watch a film of geese which explained how if one of them gets injured, they abandon the flight, go back and help their pal, then take off again. A form of motivation and stimulation? We used to watch pornos in my day! I couldn't get my head around it and I had no idea how it was going to help them so I brought it up on the radio, and I don't think Steve McClaren, the manager at the time, was too impressed because when we used to travel to the European games he'd always sit about 10 yards away but after that he wouldn't talk to me. I think watching the video was the doing of Bill Beswick, the sports psychologist McClaren installed as his assistant. Whenever Beswick called a meeting Alen Boksic, the Croatian international, was always last in and used to sit at the back, so Bill decided to do something about it. He moved the one remaining seat from the back of the room to the front, so that Boksic would have no option to sit at the front. Sure enough Boksic came in last, looked for a seat at the back, saw there wasn't one and headed for the only remaining chair at the very front….

then picked it up, carried it to the back and sat down there!

As I've mentioned before, I've made a few trips to Singapore with Gibbo and the boys to play in the veterans' tournaments over there, and as you can imagine we always had a few laughs there too. At the end of one tournament we were in the bar and John Hendrie told me that Viv Anderson was canvassing for me to be voted worst player of the tournament – and the forfeit was having to wear a big, ginger wig. Anyway, the lads decided to turn it around and we all voted for Viv. So there we were in a posh hotel for the presentation ceremony suited and booted, and Viv spent the whole night with a big, ginger wig on. To make it worse there were big screens up as well, and you could see people looking and wondering what in earth was going on.

At least I was fit enough to play for the old boys' team. On one occasion when I enrolled at a new doctors' surgery I was asked to jump on the scales to be weighed. As I took my clothes off the nurse said "You've obviously looked after yourself" – but as I stepped onto the scales she looked at me again and said "You're on the borderline of obesity." Borderline of obesity? I was 14 and a half stone at the time! That night on the radio I recounted the tale and demanded a set of scales be brought into the studio. After all of us had a weigh-in I announced I was going on a strict diet and asked the listeners to call in with any ideas or potential remedies.

Suggestions included a celery diet, the Atkins Diet, lemon diet, water diet and so on. Then one guy came on and said the only way to beat the bulge was the grape diet. He went on to say he owned a fruit shop and that he was going to deliver a box of his finest produce. Sure enough a couple of days later three individually addressed boxes turned up at the radio station reception. I opened mine to reveal a selection of huge black and green grapes as promised, Eric Gates opened his to find apples, oranges, pears, bananas and strawberries inside, but when Malcolm Macdonald opened his, it was full of cabbages and turnips. Needless to say, he didn't take his box home.

Yes it certainly is a funny old game and whether I've been playing, on the radio or out with the lads, I've certainly had a lot of laughs thanks to football.

The dirty deed in Binns window

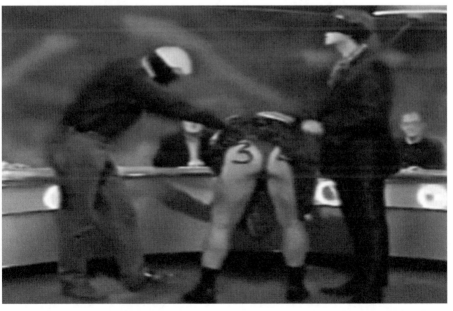

Appearing on They Think Its All Over being touched up by
Jonathan Ross and cricketer David Gower

A LITTLE
RESPECT

I'D like to think I was a successful player during my time at Middlesbrough but I've never asked for any preferential treatment whenever I've been back to the club – I'm no better than anyone else. I've never wanted the red carpet rolled out for me, just to be treated with a bit of respect, as anyone would. But there have been occasions I've visited the Riverside Stadium that have left a sour taste in my mouth.

One matchday afternoon while I was working for Century I'd walked to the ticket office to collect my tickets and, because I was in no rush, I stopped for a while and chatted to a few people instead of going straight back out. It was all nice and friendly but suddenly one of the safety officers came in through the back door, looked at me and said "You, get out of here now," and in a very aggressive, abrupt manner tried to belittle me in front of people I knew. There was no need for that, he came at me like I was some kind of rogue who had broken in or something. I wasn't going to take that and I replied "Who are you talking to, you f***ing prick? Do you think I broke in here? I was invited in!" I said my piece then calmly turned away and headed out of the door. But before I left I turned around, pointed to him and said "By the way, no f***er will remember you in 10 years' time!" Somebody who witnessed this tipped the media off and the following day I received a call about the incident but I told them I didn't wish to get involved and that I had no comment to make. Steve Gibson, the Boro chairman, thanked me at the time for saying nothing and when I arrived at the ground for the next match the safety officer in question came over and said "I owe you an apology." He shook my hand, and that was it. I don't know whether someone had told him he should do it or whether he'd sat back, reflected and decided to do it off his own bat but at least he had the balls to do it.

Ali and I used to have a ritual of walking around the pitch before we set our gear up and went on air. On the day of the Everton game in September 2000 we'd done this as usual but because we'd arrived early we had gone in without actually picking up our press passes. By this time Boro had built a pagoda on the edge of the car park and this was where the press now had to collect their tickets. We'd been at the ground for about an hour or so when I went off to collect our passes but after walking through a side door next to the main reception area I realised it was pouring down with rain. I didn't have a coat on and I didn't want to get my suit wet so I did a U-turn. The door had closed behind me and I was blocked from going in so I walked up to the next door instead. On the door was a steward who I always used to pass the time of day with whenever I saw, so I said hello and told him I was going back up to the gantry because I didn't want to walk through the torrential rain to the ticket office. There didn't seem anything wrong with that but instead of letting me through he put his hand on my shoulder and said "Where are you going?" I told him I was going back to where I'd just come from but he was having none of it. "Not through my door, you're not," he barked at me. "Your door? I think you'll find it's Steve Gibson's door," I told him. I couldn't believe it! He knew I was there to do my job with Century so what did it matter which door I went through? I hadn't gone to the Riverside to stand out in the rain all afternoon so I went back in through the main reception and back up to where I'd left Ali. On the following Monday morning I was at the Boro TV studios and when Ali arrived he gave me a letter from Dave Allan, the club's communications manager back then, who said I had been using foul and abusive language to one of the stewards and that he'd be asked to write to me on behalf of the club's operations department.

The letter reminded me that the club had introduced a new matchday system for members of the media which meant that everyone, whether they had season passes or not, had to collect tickets from the new booth and then access the ground via the new press entrance in the South West Corner. But it added: "On Saturday, however, I am told you used obscene language against a security officer who asked you to sign in, and that you then informed him you would get in through another door." Now that's a bare-faced lie because he didn't ask me to sign in, he just told me I wasn't getting in through that door. "You then informed him you would get in through another door," continued the letter and that was right, I did. "Whilst I am obviously aware that the majority of staff know your face as a former player and high profile media pundit," it went on, "I trust you will understand it is unfair to have one rule for one and another rule for everyone else. You know that you are always welcome at Middlesbrough FC," – well I'm glad that was in writing because I hadn't always felt like that – "and I hope you will agree we have an excellent two-way relationship. However any repeat of Saturday's actions is likely to see the matter taken out of my hands."

I left Ali at the studio, drove straight to the Riverside and marched into reception. I asked the receptionist if Ron Turnbull, the club's safety officer, was there but before she could answer I could see him in his office so I went in, threw the letter on his desk and said "What is this shite?" If the steward had politely pointed out that he couldn't let me through and suggested I use a different door, I could have perfectly understood it, but the way he said it was out of order. I wanted him to get the guy at the centre of the situation in so we could have it out there and then but he wouldn't do it so I headed back off to the studio. Sometimes people want to talk to you like a dog but when they hear it back, they don't like it. Talk to me nicely and I'll talk to you nicely. Abuse me and I'll abuse you. OK I called the guy a prick, but that was only because of the way I'd been spoken to first.

While working for Boro TV there were a number of people who didn't like my opinions and one of them was Keith Lamb, then the club's chief executive. He was there as an accountant when I was a player, I know him personally and I've been on holiday to Singapore and Hong Kong with him so I would have thought that if he had a problem with me, he would have confronted me face-to-face or by telephone. However I should have known better. I've always had my opinions, I was no different as a player. Referees are like the Freemasons, when they're in their own environment they don't say anything, but when they're out of the industry they're on TV or the radio and you can't shut them up, but I was the same when I was a player as I am now. I always gave my frank and honest opinions on the radio and on Boro TV but unbeknown to me, Mr Lamb went to my employer, Peter Wilcock of NTL as it was at the time and wanted to get me sacked. Now for a start it's illegal to go to someone else's employer and get someone sacked, but it didn't stop him from trying it on. Peter Wilcock, however, was a strong character and in return he told Mr Lamb "If you're going to pick my team, I'll pick yours!" A weaker manager could have crumbled but Peter backed me up and stuck with me despite getting hassle from the so-called big boys.

When I heard about this I decided I needed to have my own say, so I made an appointment to see Mr Lamb. On the day of the meeting I put a good suit on, went to his office at the Riverside and kicked off by saying "Do you want to start or do you want me to start?" He decided to go first and told me I was one of them, that I was welcome to go anywhere in the ground or the training ground and that I was "in the huddle." Whoaaa, I don't think so! I stopped him right there and told him I wasn't one of them and I certainly wasn't in any huddle. I told him I was an ex-player and a fan and that my opinion was right up the middle, I didn't favour one side over another and that it was all purely opinion and gut instinct. He might not agree with my opinion but were we living in Soviet Russia or something? Were we in a society where everyone had to be told what to think? No, of course not! In any case the club didn't pay me for my opinion so there was no need for us to both have the same views.

So that was that, we both had our say and I carried on as normal. Then I was accused by the club of saying during a live commentary that Bolo Zenden had cheated while playing for Boro against Manchester City. I'm sure on the back of my comments Ali was banned from doing interviews with the players for a few weeks. I was none the wiser until Ali told me his predicament, and when I heard the reason behind his ban I instantly apologised to the club as it wasn't meant in that context, and certainly not the way the player and the club were portraying it. I was describing Bolo's positioning while in midfield -instead of tracking his opponent on the defensive side he was gambling and letting his player drift, hoping that we would win the ball back and his opponent would be caught out.

I was talking from experience as I played the midfield role in my early days and I cheated regularly during that period. In fact one of my former managers, Bill Livingstone, once said "Bernie, you are the only guy that can score three goals from midfield and your opponent, the guy you are marking, scores four in the same game." Obviously I could have used a better word to describe Bolo for not picking up his opponent, buts that's why I apologised. If I thought he was out and out cheating, rest assured there would have been no apology.

The 2006-07 season ended with a 3-1 win over Fulham which was a great way to go into the summer break so we were all on a high. After the game I was coming down the stairwell when I spotted Mr Lamb talking to Mark Viduka, who had scored a couple of goals that afternoon but hadn't signed a new contract. I had a brief conversation with Viduka and told him well done on his performance but Mr Lamb didn't even look at me. I was due to go to Singapore with Mr Lamb, Steve Gibson and a few other Boro old boys on the Wednesday for a seven-a-side tournament, but on the Monday I received a phone call from Ali Brownlee saying that Mr Lamb had demanded a tape of our show from the Fulham match. I couldn't understand why – we'd won 3-1, we played well and there wasn't any criticism on the phone-in after the game. But from what I can gather what seemed to have upset him was my answer to the question "What does the club have to do for next season?" My reply was "Clubs have to look after the fans a bit more. They get Sky TV money, season ticket money and then a lot of games are switched, which doesn't suit the paying public." For example if a northern club's game in London is switched from a Saturday afternoon to a Monday evening, that's not good for the fan who wants to go, but the club still gets money for being live on the box. The clubs get the best of both worlds. At no point did I single out Middlesbrough, I was clearly talking about clubs up and down the country, otherwise I'd have said "The club" instead of "Clubs" but from what I could gather it was this that Mr Lamb had taken exception to.

Given the fact I was due to go away with Lamb and the chairman in two days' time I was anxious to get the matter cleared up so I phoned Dave Allan and told him I wanted him to get Lamb to call me as a matter of urgency. I told him that if Lamb didn't call me he could shove the Singapore trip up his arse, and he never did get in contact so I didn't go. It was a free trip – I'd been before and we were looked after like kings but there was no way I could go with that hanging over us. I wanted him to tell me face-to-face what the problem was so we could all go and have a good time without there being a bad atmosphere. After the chairman and Lamb returned from Singapore, Century lost the commentary deal. After 10 consecutive seasons summarising, five cup finals, two years of flying around Europe for UEFA Cup matches, over 500 games and a New York Festival award we had lost out to the BBC.

Over the years I played for Middlesbrough and Ireland in the Masters six-a-side tournament on a number of occasions at various venues including Newcastle, Belfast and London, and I always loved it. The last time I represented Middlesbrough was in something called the Premier League All Stars which was a charity tournament in Greenwich screened live on Sky One in September 2007. Every Premier League club entered a 10-man squad comprising four former players, three celebrity supporters and three ordinary fans. I was one of the ex-pros along with Craig Hignett, Jim Platt and Mikkel Beck while the celebrities were actor Mark Stobbart, singer Alistair Griffin and former world speedway champion and Redcar Bears captain Gary Havelock. We got to the final against West Ham and won 3-1. We weren't just delighted for ourselves but also the club's nominated charities, Teesside Hospice and the Butterwick Children's Hospice who each netted £50,000 as a result of our victory. Several weeks after the tournament the charities organised a dinner at the Riverside where we would present the cheques. All the players were present... except me. The reason was that the club wouldn't let me broadcast there for one night only. I wouldn't have been able to do the Legends show in Newcastle and then drive back to attend the dinner so I asked if, as a one-off, I could broadcast from the Riverside to enable me to do both. The answer was no. I could understand them not wanting me to broadcast on a matchday because the BBC had paid for the exclusive rights to do that, but this was a charity event to celebrate something I'd done representing the club. The club told me it was because the BBC didn't want me to do it but I went and confronted their matchday team in the press lounge at the next available opportunity and they told me they knew nothing about it.

Also that year the local paper, the Evening Gazette, ran a competition over the summer months for fans to name their top 10 Boro players of all-time. It was run in conjunction with the club's supporters' group the Twe12th Man and local schools who were to make banners of the nominated players. Before the start of the following season the top 10 was revealed – Brian Clough, George Camsell, Willie Maddren, George Hardwick, Wilf Mannion, John Hickton, Tony Mowbray, Juninho, Gareth Southgate and me. The chosen players appeared in the Gazette and on the internet and before the start of the opening game of the season I did a pitchside interview and I noticed banners were being put up at the back of the East Stand. In total nine appeared and the 10th was a Midddlesbrough crest – no guessing which player was missing. That's right, me. It was a petty act.

Since then, though, there has been a change in attitude – a more common sense approach, if you like – and I'm delighted. Each week I write a column in the Gazette newspaper, in which I give my opinions on the latest goings on at the club. Last autumn I gave my views on the effects of team changes and the headline – which I didn't write, by the way - was "Don't chop and change, stick with your best XI." That was actually slightly misleading because the point I was making was that I personally wouldn't chop and change – I wasn't telling Aitor Karanka, the Middlesbrough head coach, how he should do his job. By all accounts Aitor went mad and I received a phone call the following day to say that he wasn't happy. Then at 11 o'clock that night I had a text from the club's PR guy saying that Aitor wanted to meet me for lunch. I played it cool but I knew why. So when I arrived at the ground for the game on the Saturday and was making my way to the Legends Lounge, I bumped into Leo Percovich, the goalkeeping coach, and Karanka's confidante. He asked me for a word so I led Malcolm Macdonald, my guest that day, to our table and went back to see him. Leo told me why they weren't happy and I explained that the headline wasn't my doing and although I'm not a fan of chopping and changing, I wasn't telling Aitor what to do or not to do. He accepted that and invited me to a training session and to lunch – now that's a far better way to sort out an issue. It's the proper way to do it, and an example of how the club has moved on.

That particular problem wasn't of my doing but even though my opinions have got me in trouble and people have criticised me for airing them, no-one is going to gag me. My opinions haven't killed anyone and they haven't lost Middlesbrough three points. If they had, I'd keep quiet but that's never going to be the case. If I'm on the radio, I'm the listeners' eyes and if I'm coming out with drivel I'm conning them, it's as simple and straightforward as that. It's the same with my newspaper column – the readers want to read what's really happening, not propaganda bullshit.

LEGENDS COME
LEGENDS GO

AS I've mentioned earlier I always had a lot of time for Eric Gates and we were big pals during our time as colleagues on the Three Legends show, but it's some while since I've seen him.

Gatesy made his name with Ipswich Town and Sunderland before joining Carlisle and represented England twice, although our paths didn't cross much on the pitch and I only played against him in the latter stages of his career. I'm too young to have come across him any earlier! I knew all about him though. He played in the hole behind the front two and he was a great wee player who had the distinction of winning the UEFA Cup with Ipswich against AZ Alkmaar. But although our paths hardly ever crossed on the pitch I used to bump in to him at what we called Grab a Granny Night at Hardwick Hall near Sedgefield and when we teamed up on the radio we became big pals.

Like me he's opinionated and he can be fiery but charming too. I found it so easy to like Gatesy because he had everything you look for in a human being. He could be funny and daft, and we were like kids while Malcolm Macdonald was the headmaster when we were on the air.

One night when we were on air Gatesy ran out to his car during a break and came back with a box. He plonked it down on the floor but we were back on air before I had time to ask what was in it. I was pointing and gesticulating while the show was going on but he wouldn't say anything and disappeared from the studio before the show had even finished. Then the box started to move! Malcolm and I had no idea what could be inside so as soon as the show was over we opened it up – to discover a cockerel inside. Obviously we had no idea why he'd want to bring a cockerel into the studio then leave it there so I phoned him to ask what on earth was going on. "I'm only going to kill it if I keep it," said Gatesy, who lived on a farm, "I don't want it so you can have it if you want." He knew I was an animal lover and I was happy enough to take it off his hands so I brought it home. Another time he phoned me and asked if I liked cats. Actually I didn't and I'd never had one but thanks to Gatesy I ended up with two moggies that he wanted to get rid of.

When he was sacked from the Legends show I was gutted because he was a big part of the show and he was the one I bounced off.

But I kept in touch with him and every Wednesday I'd go and visit him on the pig farm where he lived and we'd have a cup of tea and a chat.

But I haven't seen him or heard from him since 2011 because – and I think this is the reason – we had a Three Legends DVD out and when we were recording it I suggested we should invite Gatesy to be on it. He'd been sacked by then but I saw it as an opportunity for him to give his side of it. He asked how much he was going to get for it but I couldn't give an answer because we didn't know how many we'd sell. He decided he didn't want to do it and that was fair enough. It was up to him. We went ahead and did the DVD and obviously he was mentioned. There was certainly nothing which came out of my mouth that slagged him off because I was a fan of Gatesy and I knew the dirty had been done on him. But he must have watched it and, for whatever reason, taken umbrage at it because I never heard from him after that.

He does talks in pubs and clubs and, after the DVD had been released, I heard he was saying things against Malcolm, which I expected, but also that there were one or two things coming out about me. I didn't take offence though, because he hadn't done me any harm. I've no axe to grind with him and he's helped me more than anybody over the years so I've got a lot to thank him for.

I'm sure that if I contacted him he'd be happy to catch up and we'd maybe sit down and have a cup of tea and a chat like we used to but we're both as stubborn as each other and neither of us has made the first move yet.

I've stayed in touch with Malcolm since the radio show ended though. We still do talks together in the North-East and he e-mails me now and then. It's a professional relationship rather than us being best mates and it will remain like that. We're different ages – he's 10 years older than me – and we've got different mindsets and backgrounds, but we work well together.

We've done talk-ins and personal appearances for years although it hasn't always gone smoothly. On one occasion Malcolm arranged for us all to do a presentation and promised there would be a few quid in it for us for doing it. A couple of months went by and there was still no sign of the money so Gatesy pulled him up on it and asked where our cash was, only to be fobbed off with some hogwash tale. A few more weeks passed and Gatesy asked him again but we were no further forward so Malcolm and I ended up having a massive ding-dong about it just before we were due to go on air. I was furious and called him a cockney c*** and he grabbed me by the lapels and had me up against the wall - we were still being pulled apart as we could hear the theme music starting up in the background. I was fuming, Malcolm was fuming, Gatesy was ruffled and although we carried on as normal while we were on air, it all kicked off again as soon as we went into the break. So it went on all night but a week later we got the money.

Some time afterwards, when Micky Horswill was on board, Malcolm arranged another function and we were told we would be getting £300 each. At the end of the night the envelope containing the cash was handed to Micky – and there was £1,200 in it. Now I was never any good at maths when I was at school but I'm pretty sure three times 300 is 900 and not 1,200! No doubt Malcolm was expecting to pick up £600 for his night's work, it's just a pity for him that Micky was handed the envelope and not him!

When I was on holiday during one close season Malcolm tried to get Micky to do a talk with him but Micky refused, telling him it was the three of us or nothing. By all accounts they had a bit of a bust-up about it, but months later while we were on air Malcolm announced he and Micky were doing a function and gave out the details for anyone who wanted to attend. I was p***ed right off because he'd made me an outcast, and I was especially disappointed in Micky because I was pally with him outside the show and he hadn't mentioned he was going to be doing it. I left the studio without saying a word but before the following night's show started, I confronted Micky who insisted that Malcolm had stitched him up and that he wouldn't do that to me. I accepted that and told him to go ahead and do the function it but added that when he got there he should ask the organisers why, as Malcolm was maintaining, they didn't want all three of us. In my own mind I was pretty certain they would have wanted us all there and the day after the function Micky phoned me and suggested we went for a coffee. I knew he had something to tell me and when we met up he explained that he'd talked to the organisers as agreed and, sure enough, they had requested the three of us but when Malcolm told him the fee would be £500 each he said he couldn't afford it. Micky told the organiser he'd been diddled because he could have had the three of us for £900 rather than the £1,000 it cost him for two. As fate would have it, I'd just received a request from a friend of mine asking for the three of us to do a talk so I didn't say a word about it to Malcolm and asked Bob Moncur to do it with me and Micky instead. Even when I confronted Malcolm over it he tried to convince me the organiser only wanted the two of them. Over the years I've got mad about situations like that but I thought on this occasion I'd get even instead and that's what I did by bringing in Bobby and it felt even sweeter.

On the subject of Bob, I did a talk with him in Hartlepool many years ago and one of the questions we were asked was about goal-scorers. I cut across him and said "Come on Bob, you were a centre-half – you know nothing about scoring goals!" Quick as a flash he replied "I know nothing about goals? I scored three in the

Fairs Cup final, I'll have you know!" That was the equivalent of the UEFA Cup or Europa League back then and Newcastle beat Ujpest in Hungary in the 1969 final, so needless to say everyone in the audience burst out laughing.

By the time the Legends finally went off air after more than 3,000 shows, the third member of the trio alongside me and Malcolm was Dickie Ord after Micky Horswill, like his predecessor Gatesy, was told his services were no longer required. Malcolm and I both played a part in Micky being taken on, as I've already mentioned, and he didn't let us down. But the beginning of the end came for him one night when we went on air and he seemed to have a bee in his bonnet about something. He seemed to me to be taking quite an aggressive tone with the callers. We took a call from a guy called Bert in Hartlepool who was a big Pools fan, a character and he'd been ringing in for years. He was one of those guys who couldn't upset you if he tried and I knew his wife and daughters – they're a nice family, as Micky knew too because we'd met them on many occasions when we'd done outside broadcasts. Sunderland were going through a tough time – no change there, then – and Bert was playfully jibing Micky about it and Micky was going along with it until, out of the blue, he said "Hold on a minute. You keep having a go at me – do you think I've had your wife and daughters?" He'd crossed the line there and I tried to diffuse the situation by jokingly asking him if it was his time of the month but inside I was thinking "You can't say that." Micky could have come back at him with something funny but instead he was aggressive and the wording was all wrong.

On the back of that we had e-mails and phone calls, and one of his daughters got in touch to say she was going to take it further and get the hierarchy at Star Radio, who aired the show at the time, involved so it was clear something was going to have to be done.

Micky had a chance to redeem himself when we were talking about players' habits and how a lot of them enjoy going out socialising when this guy came on and said "Micky, you're a fine one to talk about players. When you were at Manchester City you were just a drunk." Being called a drunk on air isn't nice thing to happen and Micky cut the guy off dead – but the caller had probably read our book 7-9-4 in which Micky actually admitted that he was drinking heavily during his time in Manchester. Bert in Hartlepool had obviously been listening and wasted no time in emailing me with a message for Micky which read "The guy had no right to say that and you did right to get him off and you deserve an apology. But sometimes the presenter should apologise to the listener." I read it out slowly so that Micky could take it all in – it was an obvious reference to the spat the two of them had. Bert had teed him up nicely, all Micky had to do was apply the finishing touch and say he was sorry for the comments he'd made about Bert's family but he didn't bite. He missed an open goal.

Malcolm was away at the time but when he came back he went through a tape of the show and said that Micky would have to go. Malcolm handled it very well actually. He met with Micky at Blackwell Grange Hotel in Darlington, sat him down and told him that although he'd still be involved in the book we had coming out that Christmas, we'd made a decision that he'd no longer be part of the radio show because of what he'd said. Micky blew his stack and put it on social media that Malcolm had just sacked him, which meant Malcolm got hammered for it. But Malcolm didn't do it in any underhand way and I'd sanctioned the decision so it was unfair that Malcolm should get all the flak. What Micky also did was get a lawyer involved, not about losing his job, but about how much he was going to get from the book we had coming out. Fine, I thought, if he wanted to play it that way – we'd divide the books out equally and he'd have to go and sell his own, which is what we did.

I've not heard from Micky since and that's sad because we got on well and I went on holiday to Australia with him three years ago. I also lost respect for him for going down the legal route and I thought that instead of sending a solicitor's letter about the book deal he should have phoned me directly – especially as I'd saved him from the sack the previous December! On that occasion he'd been in contact on Facebook with a lady who had got us involved at Koast Radio and she was offended by some of the stuff he'd written. She'd complained and Malcolm wanted to get rid of him then but I talked him round because we had no genuine proof he'd done anything serious enough to lose his job over. He was given a warning, though, so it was always going to be curtains for him if he stepped out of line again.

The day after Micky was given his marching orders I lost my da so my head was in a shed. Micky had met my father on many occasions but he never bothered to get in touch to offer his condolences. People I hadn't seen in years were good enough to say how sorry they were and I know that if it had happened the other way around I would have had the decency and courtesy to get in touch but, for me, Micky was a selfish individual and everything was always all about him and I suppose this was another indication of that. Instead of putting work issues aside, he just chose not to contact me.

BIGOTRY

COMING from Glasgow – I was only born in Paisley because all the hospitals in Glasgow were full – and still being a regular visitor, I think I'm well qualified to touch on the subject of bigotry. I'm against racism totally and the powers that be are totally right to do all they can to stamp it out in football. There's no place for it. But I'm from Glasgow and the problem there isn't racism, it's bigotry and that is on a par with racism. People have died because of it. It does my head in.

There was an incident in 2012 when Tom Adeyemi, a young Oldham Athletic player, broke down in tears because of racist abuse he was getting from Liverpool fans during an FA Cup match. I agree than nobody should have to put up with that kind of behaviour in this day and age, but if you go to a Rangers v Celtic match you'll have 50,000 fans spending 90 minutes calling you a Fenian bastard if you're playing in green and white. I've never seen a Celtic player cry. I've never seen a Rangers player cry at the sectarian abuse he'll have had hurled at him in an Auld Firm derby either. I'm a Catholic and I've been called a Fenian, a pape, a tarrier – all really offensive terms for a Catholic - and it really grates on me that bigotry is forgotten when all the focus is on racism.

In May 2011 Neil Lennon, then manager of Celtic, was attacked by a Hearts fan as he stood by the dug-out during a game at Tynecastle. The fan, if you can call him that, was later cleared of assault in court and he denied his actions were aggravated by religious prejudice. But I've always referred to Hearts as Rangers Reserves due to the fact they also have a renowned Protestant following and it's because of potential problems caused by the fact I'm a Catholic that I turned down a move to the Jam Tarts. When I was leaving Middlesbrough in 1993 I spoke to Joe Jordan, the manager of Hearts, who had travelled down to Middlesbrough to discuss a possible move to the Edinburgh club. He was trying his damnedest to convince me, but all I could think of was "Hearts, Rangers, bigoted songs…" The Hearts fans sang all the same songs as the Rangers supporters and I really couldn't see myself fitting in there. Joe told me he was a Catholic too, that the situation wasn't as I'd imagined it to be and that I shouldn't compare things to what they were like in Glasgow, but he couldn't persuade me. I'm not saying that's the main reason I didn't go there but it was a big consideration.

To this day Rangers fans still sing a song called Billy Boys which includes the lines "Hello, Hello, you'll know us by our noise, we're up to our knees in Fenian blood, surrender or you'll die." Another one goes "Oh give me a home where there's no Pope of Rome, where there's nothing but Protestants stay, where seldom is heard a discouraging word and flute bands play The Sash every day. No, no Pope of Rome. No chapels to sadden my eyes. No nuns and no priests, no rosary beads. Every day is the 12th of July." Now if that isn't offensive, dear God, what is? But at the next Old Firm game at Ibrox there will be 50,000 people singing that… while the Celtic supporters sing IRA songs in the away enclosure.

There used to be a section of Celtic fans called the Green Brigade, a group of hardcore supporters, although the club made moves to disband them at the end of 2013 following trouble during a game against Motherwell. It wasn't the first time the group were in hot water – the previous month during the club's Champions League match against AC Milan at Parkhead, the fans displayed a banner celebrating IRA hunger striker Bobby Sands. They also held aloft a series of banners which read "The terrorist or the dreamer. The savage or the brave. It depends on whose vote you're trying to catch and whose face you're trying to save." Celtic were fined

£42,000 as a result and quite rightly so because football and politics don't mix. They had a William Wallace banner at that game too. They could have made banners celebrating any number of great players who have played for Celtic over the years but instead they chose William Wallace and Bobby Sands. It's crazy.

David O'Leary told me while travelling on the team coach to an Ireland game that he had received death threats from the IRA. By all accounts they came after the then Arsenal captain had shown Prime Minister John Major around Highbury and then admitted he voted Conservative. He went on to say it was a living nightmare because he had snipers on the roof and in the garden of his family home to keep them safe and his children's playhouse was all boarded up. When going to school the kids had to be diverted onto a different route and escorted by the police. Malcolm Macdonald also told me that he was informed by the IRA he'd be shot during a game. He was advised not to play, but he did.

When I was a kid my father used to say he supported Celtic because they were the best, not because of religious reasons. In fact he was a Rangers fan between the ages of 10 and 12. And my favourite players were Kenny Dalglish, Danny McGrain and Davie Provan – all protestant. Jock Stein was a protestant too and in fact when I was growing up there was a rumour that he had a tattoo of King Billy on his chest but I still loved him anyway. Incidentally many years later I interviewed Bobby Murdoch for Boro TV and, knowing that he'd know the truth because he'd have got changed with Jock before and after matches, I asked him if it was true. His answer: "What a load of crap!"

When I left school it was very difficult to get a job, and not just because of Thatcherism but also because of my religion. Whenever you went for an interview you were always asked which school you went to and the moment you replied St… It didn't matter what came next because they knew straight away you were a Catholic and that was enough to ruin your chances. As a kid I probably didn't latch on to that but when I grew older I started to see what was happening. Why should that be the case? It doesn't matter which school you went to in England, so why should it in Glasgow?

At an earlier age I used to whistle a song called The Foggy Dew. If you haven't heard it, it's an Irish rebel song – it's about the Easter Uprising of 1916 and encourages Irishmen to fight against the British. Now I was just a kid, I didn't know what it was about and to me it was just a song I'd heard with a catchy tune, so I whistled it. But one day I was whistling it when I came in from school and my da clipped me round the ear and told me never to whistle that tune it public. He knew the offence it could cause and the trouble it could land me in, so it was a lesson learned for me.

It's not just song which can cause offence. Remember when Paul

Gascoigne landed himself in hot water by pretending to play the flute in front of Celtic fans after scoring a goal for Rangers in 1998? The gesture, a loyalist symbol, was bound to go down like a lead balloon with the Celtic supporters although in fairness to Gazza, coming from Newcastle he would probably have known a bit about the gesture but wouldn't have known the enormity of it. I interviewed him for Boro TV at Hurworth a few years after the incident and I asked him about it. He told me that not long afterwards he was driving through Glasgow when a guy in the next car had asked him to wind his window down. He didn't look threatening or anything so Gazza assumed he was a Rangers fan, but when he wound his window down the guy said "If you ever do that again I'll ****ing slash you!"

Gazza is a great guy with a heart of gold, he's just a bit mad. But other people – and I'm talking players and referees – will come out with comments south of the Border when they know exactly what they're doing. They might think they're being clever but they should go up to Glasgow and say those things, they wouldn't last five minutes. So it's important the powers that be get to grips with the problem of bigotry and treat the problem as seriously as racism.

I have a lot of respect and admiration for Graeme Souness, a former Boro player who I have interviewed by the way, who stood up against bigotry during his time as manager of Rangers. The club is firmly on the Protestant side of the religious divide and they quite simply didn't sign Catholics. Then in July 1989, thanks to Souness, Mo Johnston became the highest-profile Catholic to sign for Rangers since the First World War era. David Murray, who was Rangers chairman at the time, also deserves a lot of credit for sanctioning that, by the way. The club was formed in 1872 so how on earth did they manage to go 117 years without signing anyone who was widely known to be a Catholic? Could you imagine doing that in today's society? The signing was seen as a cardinal sin by some Rangers fans who burned their scarves and stayed away from games in protest, claiming that Johnston would never be welcome at Ibrox no matter how good a player he was. Meanwhile over at Parkhead, the Celtic fans nicknamed him Judas – needless to say he lived outside the city.

I knew Mo and I used to bump into him in nightclubs in Glasgow when he played for Partick Thistle. He was a Jack the lad type character, a ginger who dyed his hair blond. I'm sure he went back to his natural colour when he joined Rangers so it looked orange! I also remember seeing Mo get sent off in an Old Firm game at Hampden for Celtic and, after being given his marching orders, he made the sign of the cross as he trudged off the pitch. There's no doubt in my mind that was just done to antagonise the Rangers supporters and even though I'm a Celtic fan, I was thinking "What is he doing that for?"

Celtic have always been classed as a Catholic club but for me it's just a myth. Celtic were formed by Brother Walfrid as a charity to help the deprived and the poor and the Irish/Catholic link comes from the fact he was a member of the Marist Brothers, an international Catholic community. Rangers on the other hand have always been riddled with bigotry, something I came to realise at an early age when I played for an amateur team called Eastercraigs. They were to Rangers what the Celtic Boys' Club was to Celtic, with the Ibrox talent spotters using it as a breeding ground for stars of the future. That didn't bother me, I enjoyed playing for them and the manager was a magnificent guy, but when the Rangers scouts came along to watch us we were told "You Catholics needn't worry, it's for Protestants only." It's outrageous when you think about it – it's like saying "We're not interested in you because you're black."

Jock Stein was once asked. If there were two players one Catholic and one Prodestant who would you sign?" He answered "the Prodestant because I know Rangers would never sign a Catholic."

Jock was also quoted as saying. *"It's not religion that is the problem, it's the lack of religion."*

He was also quoted.

"We like to think that whoever we play we are a football team nothing more.

We are a team who will play anyone, from anywhere, from any walk of life, from any religion, from any creed." That is Celtic FC.

When I was at Morton the guy who used to pick the teams at training was Bobby Thomson, who went on to play for Middlesbrough – unsuccessfully I might add. He used to say "Pope's XI at the top, Bluenoses down the bottom." It was all done in jest, we knew that, but can you imagine a coach saying "Blacks at the top, Whites at the bottom?" There would be an outcry.

I love returning to Glasgow to see my mother and my friends, but the one thing I don't miss is the bigotry. I'm glad the people of Scotland voted no to independence in the referendum because otherwise the Union Jack would have been done away with and there'd be riots in Glasgow.

Have I ever bawled anything bigoted out? Well, yes I have actually. I was playing against West Brom with Middlesbrough and Graham Roberts was in the Baggies side. He booted me illegally in front of a packed Holgate End and I instinctively shouted "You dirty orange bastard." It was the first thing that came into my head, probably because I had memories of an on-field fracas between Roberts, when he was at Rangers, and Frank McAvennie of Celtic. Terry Butcher and Chris Woods of Rangers were also involved so it was three against one. All four of them were charged with 'conduct likely to cause a breach of the peace' although Roberts, along with McAvennie, was cleared of any wrongdoing. I also remember reading how Roberts and his wife were asked to leave a restaurant because the majority of customers there were Celtic fans and Rangers had beaten them that day. As they reached their car after leaving, a group of moronic Celtic fans tried to overturn their vehicle, which is totally inexcusable. So I was aware of his Rangers connection and that was what came into my head when I vented my spleen at him at Ayresome Park – it was a heat if the moment reaction and I didn't mean it to be a bigoted comment. It's like if you're in your car and someone bumps into you. You jump out of the car, you're angry, you see the guy responsible and you let him know you're not happy. If he's got no hair you might shout "What do you think you were doing, you baldy bastard?" If he's a bit tubby you might call him a "fat bastard." Or if he's black you might call him a "black bastard." If you're angry at someone, you've lost the plot and you come out with the first thing that comes into your head like that, does it make you a racist? I don't think so. For me that's a million miles away from being someone who genuinely holds racist views.

I came across a strong anti-Catholic feeling south of the border when I was playing for Boro. Teesside has always had a strong link with the Green Howards and Bruce Rioch invited a representative of the regiment to talk to us after training one day. We were all sent upstairs by Bruce and as we walked in we noticed there were booklets on every chair. I took a seat next to Mark Proctor and as I read through the booklet I came across the name William of Orange, which was enough to make me stop reading and put it down. A few minutes later the door swung open and in marched a little man dressed in camouflage gear with a painted face and his opening line was "Is there a Bernie Slaven in here?" All the lads pointed to the back where I was sitting and the guy continued "I hear you want to play for the Republic of Ireland, well here's your first cap." With that he pulled out a black beret and chucked it at me. What a prick! Was that supposed to be funny? It was common knowledge that a black beret was part of the IRA's uniform and that was quite obviously what he was getting at. To me, it was a slur.

The guy introduced himself as an SAS man and told us several stories about incidents in Ireland when they had diffused bombs. At the end of each story he told, he proudly proclaimed "British Army 1, IRA 0." All the time I was sat at the back thinking "What the f*** has this got to do with football?" I probably took it more personally because of the beret incident and in hindsight I think I should have hit him with it and walked out.

A few weeks later, as part of the tie-up with the regiment, the squad travelled to Catterick Garrison to play a game against the Army. As expected we won handsomely, after all we were the professional footballers. The game ended British Army 0, IRA 6 (Slaven 4). I don't really mean that about the IRA beating the Army on the football pitch, of course – I certainly don't condone killing. But the guy who came to speak to us at the club was taking the piss, there's no two ways about it. Making an obvious IRA reference to someone just because I was a Catholic with aspirations to play for Ireland simply wasn't on.

While we're on the subject of nationalities – why do the FA still insist on playing the national anthem before big games? With the amount of foreign players plying their trade over here these days, is it still relevant? Take the Arsenal v Manchester City Community Shield game in 2014: Of the 22 players in the starting line-ups, only Alex Oxlade-Chamberlain, Kieran Gibbs, Jack Wilshere and Aaron Ramsey were British. Why don't they play a song which unites everyone instead of isolates them? Play it before an England game by all means but in all other situations I'd say it's irrelevant really. In any case what are we doing singing a song that celebrates a family which says that if you marry a Catholic you'll lose your place in the line of succession? If that's not bigotry, I don't know what is. I know that will change if and when the proposed new royal succession laws come into force, but even then the reigning monarch will still have to be Church of England!

And have you heard the sixth verse of that song?

Lord grant that Marshal Wade

May by thy mighty aid

Victory bring

May he sedition hush

And like a torrent rush

Rebellious Scots to crush

God save the Queen

Rebellious Scots to crush? Hardly an all-inclusive national anthem for Great Britain is it?

And while we're taking the birthplace and culture of players into account, I'd like to mention James McClean, the Wigan Athletic winger who hit the headlines in November 2014 for refusing to wear a poppy emblem on his shirt. As is the custom nowadays, all clubs in the Football League produced shirts with a poppy emblem on the front for their players to wear on Remembrance Sunday weekend, but McClean refused to go along with it when his side played Bolton Wanderers. He'd done it before when he played for Sunderland and I supported his decision, as did Malcolm Macdonald, the last player to score five goals in a game for England. McClean was born in Derry, the scene of the infamous

Bloody Sunday massacre in 1972, and in my opinion he was right to refuse to wear a garment supporting a cause that he cannot. He was brought up close to the Bogside where 14 civil rights protesters and bystanders were murdered by the British Army during The Troubles. If I'd had McClean's background, I wouldn't have worn a poppy either. Have I personally worn a poppy? Yes I have. But I don't need anyone to force their opinion on me to respect the dead.

A former Premiership referee, who is also a Boro and Rangers fan, had his home raided by officers from Strathclyde Police's national football co-ordination unit in 2012 after a vile sectarian rant appeared on his website. No charges were brought and he said afterwards that he, his family and his associates had endured nearly 12 months of real stress and concern, but the episode left a sour taste in my mouth too. Two years earlier this former referee had been in trouble with my beloved Celtic when he described Aiden McGeady as a "cheating bastard" after an Old Firm derby and branded Neil Lennon a "hate figure". He also referred to Celtic Park as the Glitter Dome – a reference to the abuse scandal at Celtic Boys' Club and paedophile former pop singer Gary Glitter. We used to be in each other's company a couple of times a year as we both wrote columns for the Evening Gazette and were part of the paper's Talking Boro panel, which met to discuss the burning issues of the day concerning Boro. But I stopped attending because of his ill-humoured sectarian jokes and I didn't speak to him for over a year whenever I saw him on a matchday.

So, you see, bigotry is still as big a problem as racism and it's an issue that must be taken seriously.

Outside Paradise for Celtic v Inter-Milan for a Europa League game

With The Ireland Squad, Jack Charlton and Pope John Paul 11.

Trophies from my Middlesbrough career. No the TV wasn't includ

North East player of the year award 1989, Marco Gabidini,
Pop Robson.

'hen I signed for Middlesbrough, my da asked me to get a picture
ongside Wilf Mannion, I obliged.

Applauding the Boro faithful at Wembley after losing to
Chelsea in the Zenith Data System Cup.

Finally I play for Celtic in a charity game for Ronnie Coyle, myself Ronnie, Paul Mcstay, Willie Mcstay and Tom Boyd.

After being jailed for life in 1964, Nelson Mandela became a worldwide symbol of resistance to apartheid. I was a big fan of Mandela and the cause.

A long way to go to see a bridge made of Teesside steel,
Sydney Harbour Bridge.

The Trevi Fountain in Rome.

If slaughterhouses had glass walls, everyone would be vegetarian.

- Paul McCartney

Returning from Portugal with my two body guards Colin and Millsy.

L Hotel in Paris where Oscar Wilde died.

John Keats grave in Rome.

Outside the iconic Salfords Lads Club in Manchester.

Just back from a walk in the country with my Irish Setters Cara and Cinnamon.

Penny my closest companion

With Dominic and Ryan chilling on a boat in Dubai.

Last picture in public with my Da in The Legends Lounge a few years before I got the job.

Some people think I was born up this lane, the rumours are not tru

MY DA, MY HERO

I'VE always looked at my father as my brother, coach, manager, psychologist, banker, adviser and agent as well as my da. Don't forget, when I arrived in Middlesbrough in 1985 I'd signed a two-year contract with a two-year option and trebled my wages but within two weeks I was on the phone to my father saying that I was coming home. Da saw the bigger picture though and his words to me were "Well you won't be coming back here! Give yourself time, be a man for once in your life." That told me fairly and squarely! If he'd been a softer father and said "OK come home," I'd have been back like a shot and never achieved what I have, but he was telling me what I needed to hear rather than what I wanted to hear. And 30 years later I'm still living in the North-East of England thanks to my father's tough approach – I was 24 and he knew it was my last throw of the dice with regard to becoming a full-time professional footballer. Needless to say after clocking up 382 appearances, scoring 147 goals and becoming the top league goal scorer in six consecutive seasons at Middlesbrough, I've no doubt now my father's advice was sound.

The best advice he ever gave me about football was to use the inside of my foot. If you throw a ball to a kid aged two, three or four, he'll use his laces and power the ball forward. In fact it's amazing how many kids today can't use the inside of their foot when they're playing because you have to put your foot at an awkward angle but, whenever we had a kick-about, my father always did it. And whenever he threw the ball at me and I used my laces, he'd pull me up on it and tell me to use the inside of my foot. I realised how important that was as I progressed because the inside of your foot is more accurate, which is vital when you're through on goal. It worked a treat for me and when I'm coaching young players now, I try to get them to use the inside of the foot.

Although he didn't drive, over the years my da came often down from Glasgow to visit me, mostly in the summer months and I always reckoned that more people knew him than me in Middlesbrough! He would talk to anyone and there's no doubt he could charm the birds off the trees, he had so much charisma and personality. He was also the most generous individual I have ever known. For example when I moved into my first house in Middlesbrough I couldn't afford furniture but he brought plenty down for me.

As an only child, most of his attention was centred on me throughout his life but sadly three years ago my father's health deteriorated. He was losing energy due to his body not making red blood cells and, after several exploratory operations, he was found to have a heart disorder. He was in and out of hospital after that and on three occasions I had the dreaded call to say I had to get to my da's bedside because he was in a bad way.

The first time was when I was in Darlington having a cup of tea a couple of hours before I was due to do the Legends show. It was from my mother who said Da was in a bad way – the doctors had told her his kidneys were failing and that I needed to be there right away. Needless to say I dropped everything and, heart going ten to the dozen, I dashed up to Glasgow. When I arrived after a surreal journey my da's face was badly swollen because of a build-up of fluids, he was on a drip and wearing an oxygen mask. When I touched his arm he opened his eyes and the first thing he said was "What are you doing here? I told you not to come."

Because I was so eager to get up to Glasgow and see him, I absolutely flew up. Speed limits meant nothing to me as I floored it to get there as quickly as possible and I must have been doing 100 mph as I went through the borders. Suddenly I spotted flashing blue lights in my mirrors and sure enough I was pulled over by the police because of the speed I was travelling. I was going far too fast, no doubt about it and I fully expected to be booked for speeding but, to be fair to the coppers, they were sympathetic when I told them why I was going too fast. They could see I was anxious and upset, and they let me off with just a warning.

Within a week or two my da had improved considerably and was back home but unfortunately it wasn't long before he was back in hospital. This time he was transferred to the Royal Infirmary in Glasgow as the Victoria, where he'd been before, was full. When I saw him he looked terrible. He was blown up, breathless and in pain. He had a urine bag which was full of blood and when he stood up to greet me he was in pure agony. He looked so bad that if he'd wanted helping on his way I'd have done it. I knew the score. I knew he wasn't going to get better.

My visit this time was at a weekend so I took the opportunity to watch Celtic play at Parkhead the following day. They were playing Inverness Caledonian Thistle and, if they won the match, they'd be crowned league champions. I took my iPad with me and I took a huge selection of photos and videos of the game and crowd so my da could watch the scenes and hear the fans singing. But at half-time I received a phone call from my aunty saying he'd had a turn for the worse. She was keen for me to get to the hospital straight away, but because it wasn't the first time I'd had a call saying "You'd better get to the hospital", and having seen my da bounce back before, I decided to stay and watch the rest of the game. Sure enough Celtic won the game 4-1 to clinch their 44th title and I stayed to see their lap of honours and hear manager Neil Lennon make his victory speech, although I also said a prayer for my da. After that I headed off to the hospital and when I arrived I found he had been transferred to an isolated room. Again he looked dreadful but at least he was tentatively speaking. I was called into a room by a doctor who sat me down and told me my da had only hours to live. Obviously that was devastating news so I sat at his bedside until 2.30 in the morning. By that time I was so tired and emotional that I decided to go and get some sleep then come back in the morning when, hopefully, he'd still be with us. When I arrived back at the hospital the following day I was met by a heart surgeon who told me my da had days, rather than hours to live and he finished by saying "Miracles do happen, but not very often." I took time off my radio duties to visit him three or four times a day but against all the odds, amazingly he pulled himself round yet again. People were asking me how he was and I'd tell them it wasn't looking good, but then he'd get better! They must have thought I was off my nut.

During one spell in hospital he was only allowed to drink water but, not surprisingly, he was starting to get fed up of that and he kept asking me to go out and get him an ice lolly. On another occasion I'd just arrived from Middlesbrough and he asked me to go out and get him a KFC. I didn't even know he liked KFC! It was 11.30 at night but off I traipsed through the streets of Glasgow looking for a KFC, and when I did eventually find one, it was closed. By this time it was around one o'clock in the morning and I didn't have the food anyway, so I went back to my parents' house for some sleep. I'd just got in when one of the nurses phoned me – she said my da was concerned about me because I hadn't returned and wanted to know if I was OK. That was him all over, he was more concerned about me than himself. Another example of that was when I was in Dubai on holiday. I phoned him every day to ask him how he was and to tell him to keep fighting but he was more concerned about me he'd tell me "Make sure you wear a hat, that hot sun's no good for you." He insisted he was alright every time I asked, but when my mum came on the phone she admitted he wasn't well at all and that he was going back into hospital – he just didn't want to tell me.

During one spell in hospital my da was convinced that one of his fellow patients was up to no good and he told me this guy was walking up and down the ward nicking people's newspapers. That was bad enough, but one day I went into see him and he told me "Now he's nicked my f***ing underpants!" The patients all had a shower every morning and my da was convinced the ward thief had swiped his pants while he was getting himself clean. Unlikely though it seemed, there was no doubt in his mind what had happened and he was going to sort him out! My da grew up in the Gorbals, which was notoriously rough, and although his name was Hugh, his nickname was Hatchet. He never actually carried a hatchet but he was pretty handy and he'd never shirk a situation – even when he was ill. And there he was in hospital with a serious heart condition but it didn't stop him wanting to go and chin the bloke he reckoned had stolen his pants. Fortunately it didn't get that far because he found the missing pants… in his dressing table drawer where he'd left them.

During his final spell in hospital I went up to visit when I could but I was just getting my new weekend show Bernie Does Boro off the ground on Community Voice FM so the problem then was that, after returning to the North-East, I didn't see him again for a couple of weeks. Whenever my cousins or mates were with him, they'd always put him on the phone however that became less frequent as his health deteriorated.

Even towards the end of his life, he had the same selfless outlook. He even kept an ambulance waiting to take him to hospital one time because he insisted on walking the dog before going in. As he became weaker he was asked by one of the nurses at the hospital if he'd like vitamin milk on a daily basis to perk him up but, but Da was having none of it. "Give that to the old people," he replied, even though he was 79 himself at the time. He was deadly serious too. Every time I visited he would ask me to bring a pen and paper and take notes of things he wanted me to do or get. He told me to get 20 boxes of After Eight mints for the nurses who had looked after him. There weren't even 20 of them on the ward but he wanted to make sure he'd bought enough to go round. Buy your cousins and your aunty blankets for the winter, was another one. He'd tell me just to ask my mum for the money and she'd give it to me and that if I needed any cash for myself I could find some in his suit. He was the most charitable guy I've ever met, and he also used to encourage me to get involved in helping the homeless, and I've done that. I've taken part in the Big Tees Sleepout, where we all sleep rough for a night to highlight the plight of the homeless and raise funds to help, and I've been involved in other ways too. That's definitely as a result of what my father has told me I should think about.

On the last occasion I visited him, I went with my two boys, Ryan and Dominic. For the first time ever, during the time I'd visited him over the previous two years, he wasn't responding and he was in a deep, deep sleep. The last time I spoke to my da on the phone I asked him how he was and, as usual, he said he was OK but I could tell by his voice that he was far from it. I told him to hang on in there and that I'd be up the next day to see him. I did my phone-in and then went up to Peterlee for a Legends

Live show with Micky Horswill and Malcolm Macdonald and my intention was to head straight up to Glasgow after that but the rain was torrential and I decided it was best waiting until the morning. However at twenty past seven the following morning I received a phone call to say that was it. My da had passed away peacefully.

Seven has always been my lucky number – Kenny Dalglish, my childhood hero, wore No 7; Celtic won the European Cup in 1967; I wore No 7 for most of my career; I scored 7 hat-tricks for Middlesbrough and scored 147 goals for them. I won seven international caps for the Republic of Ireland… but my da also spent time in hospital on ward seven, which was a bit strange.

I actually felt relieved when I heard my father had died. Over the previous couple of months I'd even stopped praying for him. I'm religious and I do pray but I'd got to the stage where I realised I was praying for me, not him. He was a fighter, which is why he kept defying all the logic of the doctors, but there was only one way it was going to end. He was swimming against the tide, he wasn't going to get anywhere. I phoned my mum, although she had already heard the news, and I decided to keep things as normal as possible. I went for a coffee, as I always do on a Sunday, and I played five-a-side and I didn't tell anyone what had happened. My mum had plenty of people around her in Glasgow but I didn't want to be in that environment so I stayed in Middlesbrough for a few more days.

My mate Millsy, who I went to school with, suggested we went for a sauna before the funeral and, I know it sounds bizarre, but that's what we did. He picked me up, we had a sauna, got changed then headed to St Mark's Chapel which was only a street away from where my mother lives. In all my life I'd never carried a coffin but I did on this occasion, although at 5ft 11ins I was the smallest of the pallbearers. During the mass there was an opera singer and the more she sang, the more it made me and everyone present think about my da and the times we'd all enjoyed with him.

I'd told my mother that I wanted to do a reading, which surprised her because I'd never done anything like that before, but she was happy for me to do it. I wrote out what I wanted to say and I went over it again and again before the service. When the time came to read it out I stumbled a few times and the priest had to hold on to me to stabilise me but I got through it. Here's what I read:

"I'd like to say a big thank you to everyone for attending this morning – I'm sure my father is looking down and is very grateful for the turn-out. As an only son, I could not have wished to have such a terrific dad. He was a total role model – always smartly dressed, didn't drink, smoke or gamble; he was funny, charming, charismatic, generous and, of course, knew about the game of football.

"We had many arguments and disagreements along the way – mostly football related. Thankfully it was only verbal exchanges and not punches as there would only have been one winner and it wouldn't have been me.

"When I was younger I nicknamed him Jock Stein due to his dark, wavy hair, chubby features and football knowledge. On the subject of Stein, one night he received a call that Big Jock had passed away. Within 20 minutes my dad had phoned half of Glasgow to inform them… only to discover later that night that he was actually still alive and well!

"I remember joining Middlesbrough Football Club, signing a three-year contract, and trebling my wages. But after two weeks I was on the phone to my da, telling him I was coming home. His reply was 'You won't be getting in here! Give yourself time to adapt'. 'Be a man for once in your life,' he bawled. Needless to say, I didn't return home.

"At times we were like brothers as opposed to father and son. Hatchet, as he was nicknamed, was absolutely everything to me. He was my agent, minder, psychologist, advisor, banker, coach, manager and best friend. He was also the only person I have ever trusted.

"Unfortunately over the last two years he had been struggling due to ill health. Despite his deterioration, he continued to laugh, be charitable to everyone around him and never once craved self-pity.

I can only hope that I can be as good a father to my two sons as my da was to me."

I've so much to thank my da for. After leaving Morton I chucked the game in. I wasn't going to play again but he kept telling me I'd missed my chance and that I needed to start getting my act together. Without his drive and guidance I wouldn't have achieved what I have or become the person I am. Middlesbrough have a lot to thank him for too because without him I'd have gone home and I'd never have scored the goals I did for the club. My da never played football to a high standard, although he did enjoy a kick-about with guys like Paddy Crerrand in The Gorbals. Mind you he used to organise it and pick the teams so he made sure he got a game! My da introduced me to football. Like him I supported Celtic, because they pass the ball the proper way he used to tell me. He used to lift me over the turnstiles at Celtic Park and we went to the 1970 European Cup final against Feyenoord in Milan. Without him I'd never have made it, no chance.

It's because of my da that I've always been teetotal. His father was a heavy drinker and by all accounts one night my da returned home to find my grandfather verbally and physically abusing my grandmother after drinking too much. My da was only 16 at the time but that didn't stop him from setting about him. He threw him out of the house and told him not to come back and he never saw him again because his father went to Ireland and didn't return. I can't ever recall meeting my grandfather, although I think I did when I was very young, but my da used to tell me what he was like.

The last picture I have of the two of us together is in the Legends Lounge at the Riverside and now I'm hosting the Legends Lounge on Boro matchdays. Quite bizarre that, isn't it? I swear he'll be looking down and laughing, thinking "How did you end up in there on a matchday?" I still think about him all the time but I've only had one dream about him since he died.

I'm still a regular visitor to Glasgow to visit my mum, Alice. I'll admit that I don't have the same connection to her as I did with my da but we're in regular contact and it's nice to go up and see her. The cemetery where my father is buried is close by too. They say opposites attract and my mother and father were like chalk and cheese. She was the keeper of the house – she'd take care of the bills and look after me. She's not generous like my da was, in fact I'd say she epitomises Scottish people because she's so tight! I used to call her The German because she was straight-faced and dour, and reminded me of what I imagined a housewife from Bavaria or somewhere similar would be like. She still likes to go to the Irish pubs in The Gorbals on a weekend though and have a good old sing-along to the traditional music they play there. She had no interest in football, I think she only ever came to watch me play three times, but she's always been a great mother. I recall her telling my dying father that she would look after me and she has.

One of my mothers requests was to get rid of my da's clothes. I remember when my uncle Jimmy died in Ireland, me and my da burnt all his clothes. Instead of burning my da's clothes I have kept most of them.Round my neck I also proudly wear a locket with his hair in it.

My mum it has to be said has coped well since his passing. She has had a hip opperation aged 80 and moves better than me. She has decorated most of the house and bought new furniture. Her attitude and approach would put younger people to shame.

My da 'Hatchet' aged 22

My da far left posing with his mates, in front of a Whiskey sign altougfh he never touched a drop of alcohol.

Sitting on my da's knee while on holiday.

Hatchet posing with his crombie on a winters day.

PR OWN
GOALS

AS I mentioned in the previous chapter, there seems to be a refreshing, new approach at Boro these days and I'm absolutely delighted to be back at the club, hosting the Legends Lounge on a matchday. I'm grateful for that too, but over the years I've certainly seen a few PR own goals at the Riverside Stadium.

Do you remember the letter that went out to season ticket holders telling them to be quiet when they were watching the match? I was playing five-a-side one night when one of the lads I played with came over to me. He'd been a season ticket holder for many years and started telling me about a letter he'd received from the club. I couldn't believe what he was saying and even when he pulled the letter out of his pocket and showed me it, I still thought he was winding me up. The letter was from Sue Watson, who was the safety officer at the time, and it read:

"I am receiving more and more complaints from our fans about both the persistent standing and the constant banging and noise coming from the back of the stand. Please stop. Make as much noise as you like when we score but this constant noise is driving some fans mad."

So there you have it – sit down and be quiet when the match is on! What an absolute farce. The fans who make a noise and get behind the team do a great job of creating an atmosphere, which is exactly what the players want and need when they are out on the pitch. The reaction from the fans and the media was obviously one of shock, dismay and disbelief and the club moved quickly to put out a statement explaining the letter was in response to fans moving from one section to another and admitting that it could have been misunderstood. "The fans' backing is absolutely essential and we would never discourage passionate support," it went on – but there's no doubt it was a massive PR own goal. Being a hot topic we discussed the issue on the radio, and you don't need two guesses to imagine what the response was like from our listeners.

Another issue I brought up on the radio was the club's statement that fans weren't allowed to take a banner to the game unless it was on an official 'flag night'. Oh, and they had to be fireproof too. What a load of hogwash! The point I made on the radio in response to that was "Have you ever seen Anfield on a European night?" Or Celtic Park? There are thousands of banners being waved all around the stands, all of them declaring the fans' love for their club and adding to passionate match night atmosphere. Are you telling me they are all fireproof? For that matter is the big Steve Gibson banner you see at the Riverside fireproof? Has anyone gone up to it with a lighter and tested it? And where do you stop? You can buy all manner of clothing, hats and scarves in the club shop – have they got to be fireproof too?

Another big talking point we got our teeth into on the show was in 2003 when Boro fan Adrian Carr fell asleep in his seat during a game against Arsenal. Incredibly he was convicted of being drunk in a sporting arena and was given a two-year conditional discharge and ordered to pay £150 costs. I invited Adrian onto the show and it was obvious the poor lad had been hard done by. I was definitely on his side when he joined us on the phone-in. He never disputed the fact he'd had a few pints of beer - which the club sell on a matchday in their bars at the ground - but he hadn't been drinking excessively and was quite simply tired after being at work that morning. And if he was worse the wear, shouldn't the club be accountable for selling him more booze if he'd been buying it at one of the stadium bars? Adrian told us he felt the stewards had over-reacted, that he wasn't violent and hadn't shouted or sworn at them.

Thankfully he took it to appeal and the conviction was over-turned. "It is the right of every Englishman at a football match to fall asleep if they want to," Judge Michael Taylor said at Teesside Crown Court. "This is a prosecution that should never have been brought." Spot on your honour! Boro were getting hammered 4-0 and he was slumped in his seat but so what? If you fall asleep in an armchair in your living room during a match you've lost interest in, do you get arrested? Of course you don't. Take a look around a cricket ground during the summer months. There's always people asleep, although that doesn't surprise me because cricket's a boring game! They all drink at games too. If I'd been in Adrian's situation, I'd never set foot in the Riverside again.

I actually said on the radio that the Riverside had become like Colditz because that's what it seemed like. Don't drink, don't shout, make sure your banners are fireproof… In years to come, I swear they'll strap you to your seat and gag you. You'll have to put your hand up if you need a pee and they'll escort you to the nearest loo and then, after 90 minutes of play they'll unstrap you and let you go – quietly, of course.

Football fans used to go to games to get rid of their frustrations. The working man would slave away for 50, 60 or 70 hours a week to put food on the table for his family and then at the weekend he'd go to the game and shout, bawl and scream to get it all out of his system. You can't do that at the Riverside or you'll get arrested!

In February, 2006 a disgruntled Boro fan jumped the advertising hoardings and threw his season ticket at Steve McClaren, who was manager at the time, during a 4-0 home defeat by Aston Villa. The fan, Mark Davison, was hit by a £300 fine in court but the club returned his season ticket to him. Adrian Carr on the other hand had his season ticket taken off him and it wasn't given back to him until the following October, five months after the season had finished. How is that right? All he'd done was fallen asleep whereas the other guy had climbed over the hoardings and gone up to the dug-out – which is illegal – yet he was given his season ticket back. That's an injustice to me, and bad PR.

And it goes on. Boro fans in one part of Teesside were left up in arms in 2009 when chairman Steve Gibson told a BBC Tees phone-in "The majority of people in Stockton support Sunderland." Steve McClaren said the Boro fans needed educating – that went down like the Titanic. Keith Lamb hit the headlines when he said season ticket holders didn't matter and that the town would get the team it could afford. The public were told that Gareth Southgate had signed a new contract and then Mr Lamb joined us on the Legends show and dropped a clanger by saying he hadn't signed it – in the event he put pen to paper two days later. And Tony Mowbray – who, like Gibbo I'm a big fan of, by the way – told the press he was more interested in the club's hardcore fans than those who stayed away. Now this was at a time when attendances were dipping alarmingly and just 12,793 had watched a 1-1 draw with Huddersfield at the Riverside. Sorry Mogga, but that's not good PR.

And there was the signing that wasn't. A press release was issued during a pre-season friendly against Newcastle announcing that Keith Gillespie had completed his £3.5m move from the Magpies. The problem was that he hadn't! It turned out that his medical showed up an ankle injury and the club's faces must have been as red as the team's shirts when Newcastle issued a statement the following day which read:

"The announcement by Middlesbrough Football Club regarding Keith Gillespie yesterday was regrettably more than premature. Although not fully recovered from injury, it is true that Keith Gillespie held preliminary discussions with Middlesbrough over the weekend regarding a possible move. The Teesside club have said they are unhappy with the fact that the player was not yet fully recovered from the injury that he received before the FA Cup final. Newcastle expect the player to return to the squad shortly and will continue to have contract discussions with him."

I'd said for years that Gibson and Lamb were an autocratic partnership and that it needed someone to get in between them and inject some new ideas, maybe some money too. Maybe then situations like these would be avoided. I put these thoughts forward in my Evening Gazette column in November 2010, and six months later Mr Lamb was gone.

Don't get me wrong, Mr Lamb did some fantastic things for the club, many of which he never got the credit for, and he also took the flak some big decisions which weren't so good – the biggest one being the Three Points saga. As every Boro fan knows, the club failed to fulfil their Premier League fixture at Blackburn in December 1996 because of a lack of available players, a move for which they were deducted three points. If they hadn't had those points taken away they'd have stayed up, but as a result they were relegated. It's true that the club had earned enough points to stay up before they had three of them taken away but if you look at the situation objectively and ask who was in the wrong, there's only one answer. We as a club were in the wrong. We never took the responsibility to put out a makeshift team and play the game and we should have done. That game should have been played, even if our team had been made up of stiffs and young boys – anyone! Lamb took the flak for that call but it must have been a collective decision, the chairman, the manager and everyone else would have known about it. What I'll also say about that situation is that on the evening after the game should have been played there were six or seven players supposedly unfit to play in the Tall Trees on a night out. I know because I was there too and I saw them. If I was a reporter for a national newspaper, I'd have had that story on the front page. I couldn't believe what I was seeing. They'd called the game off because there was a bug going around, yet here were players deemed unable to play a game of football but fit enough to go out for the night and have a few drinks.

Since then Neil Bausor has replaced Lamb as chief executive and he's a fresh face with fresh ideas. He's younger so he's more modern in his outlook and he's just what the club needed.

WHO'S THE BOSS?

FOR the best part of 20 years my late father encouraged me to go and get my coaching badges and I did take some steps towards that– but a career in management isn't for me.

I did my preliminary course and I got my UEFA B badge – which is more than Gareth Southgate had when he was appointed Boro manager - and I was meant to go for my full badge but I didn't because I was disillusioned. When I did my UEFA B, the practical was no problem because it was about techniques, it was out on the field, talking about and showing players what to do which was fine. But when you get in to the classroom, you're bogged down with theory – theory about things that have nothing to do with football! I thought it was a load of junk. I just didn't really get it, and there were more teachers than footballers doing the course I was on and they were always going to sail through it because they're used to reading jargon. The people running the courses used words that only Malcolm Macdonald would understand! You needed a dictionary to see what some of the words meant. Bill Shankly once said that football is a simple game complicated by idiots and I thought of those words as I was listening to some of the stuff they were coming out with.

I had to go to York City for a course at the next level which was run by a guy called Gordon Staniforth, who played for York, Hull, Plymouth, Carlisle and Newport. One of Gary Pallister's mates, Phil Dinsdale, did the prelim with me in Acklam and he was keen to do the UEFA B badge too, so when I phoned up to enrol on the course I asked for both our names to be put down. The voice on the other end of the phone said it was no problem me going but the course was strictly for ex-footballers only, so Phil wouldn't be allowed to attend. I thought it was a bit strange, especially since there were so many schoolteachers on the prelim course, but it was set in stone apparently and there was no way Phil would be able to join me in York. I broke the news to Phil, who was naturally disappointed, and I travelled down on my own to the course. When I got there I looked around and saw some familiar faces, among them former Sunderland defender Gary Bennett, one-time Manchester United and England winger Lee

Sharpe and a few Hartlepool United lads I knew too. But there were also a couple of guys I didn't know. They didn't look like footballers so I was intrigued to find out who they were. At the start of the day everyone had to stand up, introduce themselves and say a little bit about their background, and when it came to the two unfamiliar faces the mystery was solved. They were both policemen. What on earth gave them the right to be there if it was supposed to be a course for footballers only? That summed it up for me and I didn't go back after that.

So that's when I decided I wasn't going to get the qualifications that any would-be manager would need to have although, to be honest, I think I'd make a good boss. I can talk to people, I'm not intimidated by anybody, egos or statuses don't bother me and I'm not influenced by anybody. Maybe I was a bit of a handful when I was a player because of my opinions but I never murdered anyone! I didn't drink, I didn't smoke, I was as fit as a butcher's dog and I scored goals. That's why I can't understand why Middlesbrough let me go when they did in 1992. I'm not saying I'd have kept the club in the Premier League but with my goalscoring record it was possible. If you can't man-manage a player you need to go on a course to learn how to do it. Treat me right I'm no problem, but start mistreating me I'll think "Hang on there's an injustice here, I'm going to fight it." These are things that are important when it comes to being a manager and if I was a team boss I'd want a few characters in my side, not just stereotypical bores, because it brightens the place up. You don't want a team of choirboys and angels, you want a few devils in there. I've watched Middlesbrough over the years and I think we've been too nice in recent times. You don't see anyone dishing out a telling off or a rollicking, but you need that because it's healthy.

One of the most important skills a football manager needs is to be able to use the right method to get the best out of his players and assert his authority in the right way on and off the pitch. It might be an arm round the shoulder, it might be a right old rollicking or something in between – the key is to know which approach will work best. Bruce Rioch was a master of it. We fought like cat and dog but I loved him to bits and I respected him as a manager. I've already mentioned some of the run-ins I had with him and another example of the way he worked was when we were away with Middlesbrough, staying in a hotel in Dartmoor. After we'd been down for our evening meal Gary Pallister and I walked up the creaky staircase to our room. On the way up we noticed there were a pair of big 6ft curtains covering a huge window and although we were well into our 20s we sensed an opportunity for some schoolboy fun. We'd seen Dean Glover go into his room and thought it would be a great idea to climb up onto the ledge, which was a good 6ft up, hide behind the curtains and jump on him when he came past again. We obviously couldn't see anything because we were behind the curtains but when we heard a door go the pair of us jumped out like Batman and landed on our victim... who turned out to be Bruce! And you know what?

He didn't flinch. If someone had leaped out on me from 6ft up I'd have jumped a mile but he just shrugged his shoulders and walked away. It was harmless horseplay, there was no point in him reading us the riot act so he didn't. Bruce was everything you wanted in a boss – he was your manager, coach, physio, minder, psychologist – he was a father figure. He'd always be telling me to do this and do that in training and one day I snapped back at him and asked him why he was always on my back. He just stayed calm, pulled me aside and said "It's simple – when I'm not shouting at you it means I've lost interest in you and you'll be out of the door."

Whenever you saw Bruce for the first time on a morning he'd always ask "How are you today?" And every time your reply had to be "Great." If you said you were okay or anything like that, he'd give you a slap and say "No, you're great today!" You had to shave every day under Bruce too, and I picked up many a fine, usually £10, for not coming in clean shaven. Another time Pally and I went swimming at the local baths in Billingham and the club received a letter saying we'd been messing about – which, to be fair, we had – which earned us another fine, this time £25. The letter told us we'd been guilty of "conduct unbecoming of a Middlesbrough player in a public place". I went to a Sunderland game with Pally one night and wore a tracksuit – that was another fine because Bruce caught wind of it and said we were representing our club so we needed to be smart. Young lads with love bites he'd send home or tell to cover them up. I've honestly lost track of the amount I paid in fines to Bruce over the years but I liked his style. Everything he did was for the right reasons. I've kept all the letters sent out by Tom Hughes, the club secretary, informing me of some disciplinary breach or another and there's stacks of them! I wish I'd had as many letters from the club praising me as I did for telling me I'd be fined. There's one letter, which we all got, which informed us that if we'd put on too much beef over the summer we'd be fined £10 for each pound we were deemed to be overweight when we returned to pre-season training, another letter was to tell me my wage packet would be £37.50 lighter for showing dissent, another one was to tell me I'd been fined £30 for failing to report for treatment on time – the list goes on and on. We were on peanuts compared to what players earn these days so I must have been skint by the end of it!

When Bruce left Boro he wrote me a letter, which I've still got. It read:

Dear Mr Slaven

Having spent the best part of four years with you, I feel I ought to write and express my thanks for your efforts during that period. It has been greatly appreciated by myself and I hope that during that period you have learned a great deal more about the game of football and I know you will have improved your capabilities and abilities.

The main aspect for you now is to continue to work hard at the physical and technical part of your game and try to absorb and appreciate the game in a finer detail.

You have been a tremendous help to me personally and I would like to take this opportunity to wish you and your family every success both professionally and personally. If I can be of any assistance to you in the future, please do not hesitate to get in touch.

It was a nice touch and proof, if ever it was needed, that all the bust-ups we had were because he was just trying to get the best out of me. I still don't know why he addressed it to Mr Slaven and not Bernie, though!

One manager whose methods I didn't approve of was Lennie Lawrence. The first time he walked through the door at Ayresome Park I knew I didn't like

him. For his first team talk he sat us all down on the Ayresome Park turf and the words that caught my attention were "I'm looking for new heroes". Here he was telling guys like me, Tony Mowbray and Stuart Ripley who had taken the club from Division Three to Division One that he wanted new idols. That, for me, indicated he wanted to get the old guard out and that's exactly what he did – Mogga joined Celtic, Rippers went to Blackburn and I eventually went along with some others too. I lost respect for him instantly.

My first run-in with Lennie came when we played Bristol City away – an important game because we could have gone top of the Division One table. Just before we left the hotel he announced the team and I wasn't in it, despite being top scorer. What annoyed me most was that he didn't have the balls to call me to one side in the hotel and explain why. If I'd been a manager in that situation, it's how I would have done it. I asked Lennie for an explanation before we boarded the coach but he told me to wait until we'd arrived at the ground and he'd talk to me then. When we got there, instead of telling me in the dressing room he insisted we went out onto the pitch where everyone could see us. I told him to his face are we here for a victory tonight? We can top and you have John Gittens and Stuart Ripley on the bench. "Do you know your problem, your a ****ing school teacher."I bawled. The game ended in a draw.

But times have changed. You couldn't get away with what Bruce did these days and, to be honest, the thought of being a manager in the modern game isn't an appealing prospect. I couldn't work in an environment where people are in control of you.

I ended up in hot water last year for an article I'd written about who actually signs players at a modern day football club. Is it really just down to the manager, or does the chairman and his mates in the boardroom have a bigger influence these days? My gut instinct is that it's more than just the manager picking which players he wants at the club and I received a phone call out of the blue from Boro chairman Steve Gibson who said I'd been inaccurate. My reply was that if he talked to people other than his cherry-picked few, I'd be in possession of the full facts, but since I wasn't in the loop I didn't have that luxury. For example Gareth Southgate says it wasn't his decision to sign Afonso Alves in 2008 but Keith Lamb, the chief executive, insists he did know about it. I know who I believe. Juninho came back to Middlesbrough twice – did Steve McClaren actually want him back? Was it Tony Mowbray or the chairman who wanted Jonathan Woodgate back at the club? It's questions like these which make me convinced I was right all along.

To me it seems like it's a collective decision — it's not just the manager, or first team coach as the gaffer is known as more often than not these days, who signs players. I'm not a fan of that. If the chairman, the chief executive and chief scout all get involved in which players are going to be brought in over the manager's head, will they carry the can if it all goes belly up? Of course not! It's the manager who's going to end up losing his job, not them. If I was a manager and all these people were sticking their oar in, I'd agree to sign a contract on the one condition that if it all went wrong we all got sacked, not just me. You can argue that the chairman deserves to have a say if he's putting millions of pounds into the club but if that's the case, he's not looking for a manager is he? Sir Alex Ferguson wouldn't have stood for it. Neither would Harry Redknapp, but chairmen today are trying to groom the modern manager and shape him so they've got him where they want him. I always feel the hierarchy have a need to employ people who are weaker than themselves in the main. I think in the main Steve McClaren went against the grain before he left Middlesbrough. He was a fairly strong character who started to stand his ground but there aren't too many like him.

You have to ask, what do chairmen and chief executives know about the game? Tommy Docherty once said "You could write on the back of a stamp what they know about football," and I can see where he's coming from!

Former Newcastle, Sunderland and England forward Len Shackleton famously included a chapter called The Average Director's Knowledge of Football in his autobiography… it consisted of a single blank page! I'm in agreement with that. If you start getting involved you're undermining the people you have appointed to run the football side of things and not showing much faith in them. You should let them get on with it, simple as that.

When Gareth Southgate was manager at Middlesbrough, you'd often find him talking about accounts and Keith Lamb, the chief executive, talking about football. That seems the wrong way round to me.

Steve Gibson is probably an exception to the rule. Unlike the Glazers at Manchester United and Sunderland owner Ellis Short or Newcastle's Mike Ashley, he is a genuine fan of the football club. He was brought up in the area and supports the club he owns and has run over the years. I have got to know Gibbo and his enthusiasm and knowledge of the game is undebatable. He also loves to play the game - I would love to see any of those owners I've mentioned kick a ball, especially our Mike up in Newcastle. Our owner/chairman is unique. A couple of years back he went on record as saying he was ploughing £1m a month of his own money into the club to keep it afloat. How many other guys out there would have done that?

After Gordon Strachan's short and disastrous spell on Teesside and then my mate Mogga's stint in the hot seat, it was of vital importance to nominate the right man for the job. As I write this in March 2015, Aitor Karanka's team are sitting top of the Championship table with a great opportunity of returning to the Premier League where we belong. The turn-around at the football club in recent years has been there for all to see, not just on the field but off it too. In my opinion a gulf between the club and its supporters had developed since around 2006, when we reached the UEFA Cup final in Eindhoven. But the club now works in tandem with the supporters and listens to their thoughts, ideas and opinions. And the players acknowledge the supporters home and away, which hasn't always been the case. Karanka himself has been quoted as saying that from the tea lady to the chairman, everyone is important at this football club.

Over the years I have mentioned and heard stories about heavy-handed stewards. Fortunately all of that seems to be in the past now. The changes behind the scenes over the years in key areas seem to be working, so much so that I now host the Legends Lounge at the Riverside on match days.

Every picture tells a story, I instantly lose respect during this first team talk as Lennie Lawrence mentions he is looking for new heroes Im the only one looking away.

With the Bruce Rioch 'Gaddafi' in Odense Denmark

THE IMPORTANCE OF OPINIONS

AS I've said many times, it's important to have an opinion when you're a pundit and here is a quote that sums it up perfectly for me. I'll be honest, I've no idea who said it but it certainly strikes a chord with me:

"Deep down there are likely to be a great many people who agree with you – but for various reasons are reluctant to step forward and declare what they truly believe. The person who courts popularity usually conveys a dishonest message. A person who conveys an honest message is seldom popular."

Everyone seems to be carefully cultivated to fit into the right mould these days. Very few people seem to be gloriously opinionated, but that's what I like. I admire people who can give it both barrels, be they a king or a pauper, and I believe that's something I can do.

Whenever I've interviewed players, that's the sort of qualities I'm looking for in them. One of the players I was critical of at Boro was Abel Xavier after he failed a drugs test. The former Portugal midfielder tested positive for an anabolic steroid called methandrostenolone after Boro's UEFA Cup tie with

Skoda Xanthi in November 2005 and was slapped with an 18-month ban, though he always denied any wrongdoing, and his suspension was later cut to a year which allowed him to revive his playing career with Los Angeles Galaxy in the MLS. I spoke out about it at the time because I'm very anti-drugs and I believe that if you're guilty of such misdemeanours in football you should be banned, simple as that. When Ali Brownlee and I were in New York to collect our radio award, I received a message from Dave Allan, the Boro PR man, that Xavier wanted to see me. I've always said that if anyone has a problem with me they should tell it to my face, so I was happy enough to meet him. Our schedules meant we couldn't meet up in America but I told Dave to give him my number, which he did, and sure enough Xavier called me. We arranged to meet up at Teesside Airport and I was expecting him to take me to task about what I'd said about him. But he bought me a cup of tea, we sat down and he never mentioned it. Instead he said there were a lot of things going on behind the scenes at the club and that the lads wanted me to know about them because I was on the radio and they felt

I should be made aware. There were about a dozen games to go that season and although the European campaign was going great guns, it wasn't going so well in the league. Xavier explained how Mark Viduka and Stewart Downing were both out of contract, that there was unrest among the players and that they wanted to go to the very top with their concerns but the chief executive, Keith Lamb, kept intervening. I invited him on the show and he came on twice. I liked him. He was polite, honest and forthright and a character too.

Xavier was a bit like Fabrizio Ravanelli in that he had big opinions and he wanted the best for the club. He was a deep thinker and he was trying to better things, and I could see the value in some of what he was trying to say. Rav was very critical of the facilities when he first came, and he was right to be. I went to interview him many years later in Rome when he was playing for Lazio and when I arrived to see him there were these big, 20-foot high gates with a wall the same height surrounding the training park. When the gates opened they revealed a vast expanse of lush football pitches being sprayed with water, palm trees in between. When Rav first came to Boro it was before Rockliffe Park was built and the team was training at Tollesby Road, which wasn't much different to a municipal park, so no wonder he wanted better facilities if that's the sort of thing he'd become accustomed to in Italy!

Over the years I've interviewed well over 300 Boro greats - Brian Clough, Fabrizio Ravanelli, George Hardwick, Wilf Mannion, Jack Charlton, Graeme Souness, Bruce Rioch to name but a few. During that time only two players declined to be interviewed – Alan Peacock and Alex Smith. And only two players asked for a fee – the late, great Bobby Murdoch, my father's favourite ever player, and Spike Armstrong.

The players I interviewed were always keen to tell me it straight and, in the case of Xavier, he came to me rather than me to him. A lot of the interviews I did were for Bernie's About, one of the features on Boro TV, and not everything my guests said saw the light of day. For example I interviewed Marco Branca who, at the time, had been told by the club he was not fit enough to play. Two specialists over here had said damage to his knee ligaments was too serious for him to be kept on but his people in Italy were saying the opposite. In the end Branca sued Boro for £500,000 in loss of earnings, won the case and resumed his career with Monza in Serie B. Obviously while this was going on he was keen to open up about it in our Boro TV interview but a lot of what he said was edited out. He was critical and wanted to get his point across but clubs up and down the country – and I'm not just talking about Middlesbrough – will grind an individual down if they want him out, or at least try their hardest to, and a lot of them crumble. I've never read one single report where, when a player leaves, it's the club's fault. It's always the player's fault – and he's usually not allowed to say anything against the club once he's gone because he'll be made to sign a gagging clause in his contract before getting his settlement. Their silence is bought and I'm not a big fan of that. The people who run football clubs are ruthless, hard-nosed businessmen and everything is done for the benefit of the club. One of the exceptions to the rule was Gaiza Mendieta, of course, who stayed put and picked up his money when he was surplus to requirements. They made him train with the reserves but he dug his heels in and picked up every penny.

But if I was an agent, I'd be advising my players to move every couple of years. There's no such thing as loyalty in football so if the clubs can be like that, then so too can the players. Eventually they're going to get rid of you anyway, so you may as well do it on your terms. Look at me – I was loyal, successful, and cheap but I was forced out at Middlesbrough. And they wanted me to sign a confidentiality document to say I wouldn't speak out against the club before I joined Port Vale, but it was them who wanted rid of me. When it comes to negotiating a deal it's obviously up to the player to call the shots, not his agent and if he's happy the agent shouldn't try to force him to move against his will. But I don't see any value in sticking around until the club decides you're past your sell-by date. The players have to look after themselves because the clubs will always look after No 1.

THE NON- FLYING
SCOTSMAN

WHEN I was a kid I used to fly regularly when we went on holiday and back then stepping on the plane was one of the best parts of it. It was an adventure and I loved the buzz of shooting down the runway because it was a sure sign that fun times were ahead. I loved it.

But later in life I developed a phobia of flying which took hold on December 22nd 1988. I didn't get many days off over the festive season and with a game coming up against Everton on Boxing Day, I decided to take the opportunity to drive up to Scotland to see my parents.

Tragically the night before my journey, PanAm flight 103 was blown up by a terrorist bomb over Lockerbie, a little town just over the Scottish border, which sits right next to the A74, now the A74 (M), and that's the road I had to use to get to Glasgow. The atrocity brought down the plane, scheduled to fly from Frankfurt to Detroit via Heathrow and New York, killing all 243 passengers and 11 crew on board plus 11 more people on the ground. There is an alternative route, taking the A696 out of Newcastle and heading north via Jedburgh but I was an inexperienced driver, I'd been a licence holder for only four years and didn't know the roads very well back then. I'd also gone to bed the previous night unaware of the disaster so that meant I'd be passing the spot where the transatlantic jumbo jet had come down, less than 24 hours after it had happened.

I heard about what had happened on the news the following day as I was preparing to set off. The news bulletins were advising motorists not to travel on the A74 unless it was essential, but going to see my parents at that time because of my football schedule was pretty essential to me. There was no way I was going to call the trip off because it was my only chance to see my parents over the Christmas period so I headed off past Darlington, up to Scotch Corner, along the A66 and onto the A74 near Carlisle. As I got close to Lockerbie the police had blocked off two of the three lanes and all the traffic had slowed down. There was a massive crater in the ground to the right, military helicopters in the air and police on foot looking for bodies, smoke still rising from the smouldering wreckage and clothes strewn across the ground. It was a truly horrific sight and it really got to me. I didn't want to look, to be honest, but when you pass something on that scale first hand and the traffic is slowed down to walking pace, you can't really help it. Roofs had been ripped off the bungalows and houses next to the road, scorch marks were everywhere and there was debris all over the place. I instantly said a prayer for those people who had lost their lives and in fact I still do so every time I pass the spot.

The experience had a traumatic effect on me and it took me years to conquer the fear of flying I developed as a result. I've lost thousands of pounds in unused air tickets, I've faked injury to prevent getting on a steel bird, I've disappeared from check-in desks, I've taken Valium, I've taken boats instead and I've done a runner from a hotel room in the middle of the night all because of my phobia.

The first trip I missed was in March 1989 when I was playing for Middlesbrough who were heading off to Bermuda to play games against their national side and Coventry City, who were then a First Division club too. We'd gone down to London by coach and were staying overnight in a five-star hotel before our flight to the Caribbean the following morning but for me seven hours in the sky were a big problem and I told our physio, Tommy Johnson, I'd need some Valium to take before we went. I never drink alcohol so I wouldn't be having a pre-flight drink to calm me down and I couldn't disguise my fear, so Tommy assured me he'd get me Valium. I needed to take the tablets well in advance of take-off but despite asking Tommy before we boarded the coach and again at the hotel in London, he didn't come up with the goods. By this time the fear was building up inside me and I said to Gary Pallister, my room-mate "I'm not going." Pally to his credit did his best to calm me down but when he could see it was having no effect, he took drastic action… he phoned my father! I was 28 years old but there he was phoning my da to get him to have a word with me. Even that did nothing to change my mind so then Pally threatened to call Bruce Rioch and tell him. There was no way I was having him phone the gaffer, though, and I told him straight "If you grass, that's me and you finished." I assured Pally I'd get my head down and see how I felt in the morning but in truth I had no intention of getting any sleep. I'd roomed with Pally numerous times in the past so as soon as I heard him snoring, I knew he was out of the game and that was my cue to leave him to it. I got up, gathered my gear together and left him a note on the toilet seat that read "Have a good time with the lads big man, I'll see you when you get back."

I headed off into the night and arrived at King's Cross station, where I found myself surrounded by drunks, druggies and all sorts, and I started thinking I'd have been better off on a plane! I caught the first train to Darlington the next morning but my wife at the time, Karen, told me Bruce had discovered I'd gone and he'd already been on the phone so I couldn't be seen in Middlesbrough. I ended up staying for a couple of days with Jamie

McCreadie who was a prison officer near Blackpool but when I thought the time was right to head back to Teesside I was told I still had to stay away, so I went up to Glasgow for a few more days to try and stop anyone outside the club finding out I wasn't where I was supposed to be.

Unbeknown to me the national press were phoning Pally asking if I was with the squad in Bermuda and he just had to fudge it the best he could. When the reporters started getting conflicting stories from other players, the press soon smelled a rat, though, and before long headlines like "Slaven gets his winged clipped" started to appear in the papers.

I was living in Westbourne Road in the heart of Middlesbrough at the time and after the team returned home, Pally arrived on my doorstep in his club blazer, looking very tanned, and told me it was looking likely I'd get sacked for going AWOL. My attitude was that I'd asked for Valium tablets, the club didn't provide them so I had no option. The following day I joined the lads for training at Maiden Castle in Durham and as we were getting changed ready to start the session Joe Hunt, the kit man, came over to say Bruce wanted to see me. I headed off thinking "Here we go, I could be out of a job" but instead of an explosion from Bruce, he quietly told me to come into his office and take a seat. I still expected an ear-bashing but he remained calm throughout our meeting and said "Why didn't you tell me about your phobia?" I explained that he was a tough nut and I expected he would most probably have dismissed it as nonsense but Bruce just outlined practicalities of the situation – I'd cost the club money by not using my plane ticket and he could have taken someone else in my place if I'd told him I wasn't going to go. I didn't get the sack and instead I was fined one weeks' wages, which I couldn't really argue with. Bruce could blow up at the drop of a hat but this time he became a father-like figure and handed me a newspaper cutting about the phobia of flying and told me to get myself sorted. We played Liverpool in the next game and lost 4-0 – I blamed the lads for being away and said the sun had obviously sapped their energy!

One trip I did make with Boro came after we won promotion to the First Division in 1988, although I almost didn't get on the flight home. We all had

a bet we would beat Bradford and Chelsea, our opponents in the play-offs, which of course we did. Bruce had told us after our final league game of the season against Leicester City, which we lost 2-1 and eneded up in the play-offs, that he wanted us all to bring £100 in the following Monday and he'd put the bet on. I don't bet usually, I wouldn't know what to do with a betting slip if I walked into a bookies, but I went along with it and the rest is history. We went up and after sealing our promotion we jetted off to America. Before we boarded the bus down to London to catch the plane Bruce came round and gave us all our £1,000 winnings, and I gave mine to my wife as I already had enough cash for the trip and wouldn't be needing it in America. I made it across the Atlantic OK but when it was time to come home I threw another wobbler and decided I wasn't going to fly back. I told everyone I was getting the boat instead. That would have taken about five weeks but I was still adamant I wouldn't be flying back and started asking some of the lads if I could borrow some of their winnings to buy my ticket. So much for not needing my winnings! Since missing the Bermuda trip, however, Bruce had been aware of my phobia and this time someone told him what I was going to do and as a result Bruce managed to get some tablets for me to take and I joined the rest of the lads on the plane home.

On the same trip we had to make a few internal flights and on one of them I was in such a state that I couldn't sit down. I kept pacing up and down the aisle and at one point I was talking to a stewardess at the back of the plane. She could have been Racquel Welch or she could have had a beard like Conchita Wurst who won the Eurovision Song Contest, I really wasn't in any state to register what she looked like. It didn't take her long to realise there was something up and after disappearing for a second she came back with a wee box and produced a tablet from it for me to take. I've no idea what it was but I took it and it seemed to have an effect!

Walking out of the hotel before the scheduled Bermuda flight was just one instance on a list of missed trips. I won seven Republic of Ireland caps which possibly could have been more had I not gone to either Bruce Rioch or Colin Todd, my managers at Middlesbrough at the time, and asked them to withdraw me from the squad after being selected because I was injured or had the flu, when in fact I was fully fit but just couldn't face flying.

I remember being in the Ireland squad for a trip to Boston one summer but I couldn't even face getting on the small plane from Newcastle to Dublin so I drove to Holyhead in Wales and caught the boat instead. I'd done that a few times and the guys on the ferry let me have a sleep in my car and because I'd got to know them after doing it so many times, they actually brought my breakfast to me the next morning too. There was no avoiding getting a plane to America though so I made sure I'd swallowed some Valium. Just to be on the safe side I asked the team doctor if he had anything I could take and he gave me these things that were the size of Extra Strong Mints, and even though I had no idea what they were, I took them. I think I was higher than the plane! I was so light-headed due to my drug intake that I actually bought a Raymond Weil watch for £500 when we changed planes at Shannon Airport. When you have a phobia like this you're not just wasting other people's money, you're wasting your own too. I didn't want a watch and I've no idea why I bought it, but at least the tablets were working and I slept for the rest of the journey.

I was, of course, selected by the Republic of Ireland for the 1990 World Cup finals in Italy and that was always going to involve lots of time in the air. We had to fly to Turkey for a friendly, then take two flights to get to Malta to get acclimatised for the tournament then jet into Palermo, Sicily, Genoa and then Rome before returning to Dublin. Unbeknown to Jack Charlton and my team-mates, I had more tablets in me than Boots the Chemist by the time we'd been knocked out of the competition by the host nation in order to get me through every flight. Did those tablets have an effect on me during training sessions? Without a doubt, yes! I used to feel jaded, light-headed

and weak, especially when the searing heat hit me and the training sessions became more strenuous. But the one thing that never crossed my mind was being drug tested. The only two Republic players asked to provide a sample of their urine during the World Cup were Paul McGrath and big Niall Quinn. The first player I'd heard of failing a drug test during a World Cup was Glasgow Rangers winger Willie Johnston back in 1978 in Argentina after playing for Scotland against Peru. He was found to have taken a banned stimulant and his subsequent expulsion from the squad ended his international career – and that could have been me too in 1990 had I been tested. Valium isn't a performance-enhancing drug, it's not going to make you go any quicker but you have to declare what you're taking and I can't be certain that what I'd been swallowing as a result of my fear of flying wouldn't have resulted in a negative test, especially as I hadn't told anyone what I was taking.

At least I got to America on that occasion but it was a different matter when I was asked to go to Indianapolis to coach and play for three months after retiring and it seemed like a good opportunity. I got my former team-mate Mark Proctor involved and we purchased new passports and visas then booked our tickets to the States. Proc knew what I was like when it came to flying so the night before we were due to leave he arranged for me to take his passport and his flight documents – he knew it wasn't out of the question I'd want to do a runner but there was no way I'd stop him from making the trip. We'd arranged to meet at the Tall Trees in Yarm at 5.30 the next morning and I was there well before him. I was having a good laugh and chat with some friends but when they left it suddenly dawned on me that I was going to have to get on a plane in a few hours. I didn't want to let Proc down but I just couldn't do it. So I went up to the porter, who I knew, and asked him to look after Proc's passport and tickets while I popped out to the garage, which of course was a lie. Even he knew my flying phobia and wanted to know if I was coming back so I assured him I was, even though I had no intention of doing so. Instead I jumped into my car and drove towards Darlington just to get away from having to fly. I found a gap in the hedge next to the road and drove into the field where the rapeseed they were growing was a good eight or nine feet high. I was knackered, I was drained and I'd taken tablets too so I fell asleep in the car. When I eventually woke up and returned to the family home I discovered that the guy who had organised the venture had found out I wasn't going to be on the plane to America and had phoned all the press and the local radio stations and asked them to put out a bulletin saying I'd gone missing and if anyone could find me they'd get a signed Middlesbrough shirt! Proc made the trip on his own and phoned me on several occasions trying to persuade me to make the journey belatedly but my mind was made up and I didn't go.

Another trip I didn't make was when I was due to visit Juninho, who was playing in Spain for Atletico Madrid at the time. I'd arranged an interview with the former Boro and Brazil star for Boro TV – the plan was to watch Boro's Premier League game with Arsenal at Highbury then jet out to do the interview. I was summarising the game for Century but unbeknown to my colleagues or the listeners, I had taken a couple of Valium tablets to calm my nerves. Ali Brownlee and I did a phone-in after the final whistle then headed off to catch a taxi to the airport. But when the cab arrived I refused to get in and I told Ali "I'm not going." I could see Ali was getting worried and anxious but even though

I'd been taking Valium, I still couldn't face the flight and I went back home instead.

My fear of flying really was starting to cause problems. I remember queuing at Glasgow Airport with a mate ready to board a flight to Cyprus for a holiday and as we started to approach passport control I did a U-turn and went back to my car. I'd also paid a few quid for a five-day break in New York but I woke up on the morning of the flight and decided I wasn't going so I ended up in Amsterdam via the ferry.

After my phobia became known, people would often ask if I'd ever flown and of course I had. As well as going to Spain regularly as a kid I've flown all over the world as a player – America, Germany, Canada, Poland, Portugal, Sweden, Hong Kong, Austria, Cyprus, Denmark, Gibraltar, Hungary to name but a few of the countries I've jetted into. So how did I achieve it? With great difficulty is the answer to that. To be perfectly honest the whole flying scenario was bizarre. When I knew I was going abroad and I'd booked a flight I was excited but in the few days leading up to it I was at my most vulnerable to my phobia. That's when I started becoming nervy and agitated and having sleepless nights. If I made it as far as the airport and boarded the plane I had a certain ritual – with sweating palms I'd sit as near to the front of the aircraft as possible because there is less turbulence at the front, I'd put my earphones on so I didn't hear any of the safety information they read out and I'd avoid sitting next to a window.

So what was I scared of? The obvious thing was crashing. My biggest fear was the engines cutting out although all the while I was aware that flying was still the safest form of transport and my chances of being involved in an aircraft accident were something like one in 11 million, while my chances of being killed in a car were one in 5,000. I remember coming back home from Middlesbrough's UEFA Cup game in Ostrava in the Czech Republic and jumping straight into my car to drive to the local shop. I was stuck behind a lorry on a country lane when all of a sudden it started to reverse without warning and put a hole in my bonnet. I was far more likely to come to harm in an incident like that than I was in a plane. But I drove up to Newcastle every day to the radio studio and never worried once about crashing, it never even entered my mind, but the difference is that when I'm driving, it's me who's in control.

But a fear of flying is a phobia and a phobia is irrational. It's something that had to be sorted out once and for all. Alcohol and tranquilisers weren't the

answer, although I've always been teetotal. Mind you, there was one occasion when I did have a drink as a result of my phobia. Along with the rest of the Middlesbrough team I was flying back from Kennedy Airport in New York but our take-off was delayed while we were on the runway and I was starting to become a wee bit nervous. Everyone had been given a complimentary drink and Gary Pallister, who I was sitting next to, had a Bacardi and Coke in front of him. He was deep in conversation with whoever was on the left of him and, with my anxiety growing, I just picked his glass up and downed the contents while he was talking. When Pally turned to pick his glass up he couldn't believe it was empty. He wanted to know who had necked it, although he didn't suspect for a second it was me because I was teetotal!

The answer to conquering my phobia definitely lay elsewhere, so I decided to do something about it. When I first joined Middlesbrough I went to the Park View Medical Centre in Claireville for my medical and I went back there to see Jean Brady, the hypnotherapist I also went to see about my depression. Because of my depression I was starting to look like Jack Nicholson's Randle McMurphy character in One Flew Over the Cuckoo's Nest so I had regular appointments with her. She had a lovely, calm voice she dimmed the lights, I requested a blindfold to put on and she talked about all the tranquil things in life. And it worked. Since then I've flown to Spain, Portugal, Dubai twice and even Australia and I swear to God I haven't needed to touch any tablets.

The Malaysian Airlines flight 370 from Kuala Lumpa to Beijing went missing a few months before we went to Dubai and then the night before we came back, another Malaysian Airlines plane was shot down over Ukraine. If that had happened a few years ago I would probably have not got on the plane, but these days I board an aircraft knowing the odds of coming to any harm are next to zilch and knowing that I'm going to arrive at my destination safely. I think logically about it, like a normal person does – after all I'm sure the pilot doesn't walk into the cockpit and think "We're going to crash today!"

If you'd have told me ten years ago that I was going to fly to Australia I'd have said you were off your head but I did it without any problem, and in fact recently I've started to feel that buzz again when the plane is shooting down the runway.

With my da as he lifts me off the plane after touching down in The Isle of Man.

A LUCKY
ESCAPE

IN February 2012 I moved into rented accommodation in the grounds of Gisborough Hall, which if you don't know, is a lovely country house hotel on the outskirts of Guisborough, around 10 miles from Middlesbrough – and both my partner and I very nearly paid a very heavy price for it!

We'd been in the place for about two days and it was a freezing cold Sunday night, so I decided to light a coal fire to warm us up at about half past nine in the evening. I put a bag of coal on the fire and then settled down to watch Match of the Day 2. I'd never lit a coal fire before but I soon got it going, although the smoke was billowing inwards rather than up the chimney and it was getting in my eyes. So instead of watching the TV downstairs we went upstairs and watched it in bed instead, before going to sleep.

Now once she is in bed, that's it – she never usually gets up to go to the toilet or anything. But on this occasion I heard her getting out of bed and it was pitch black so I shouted out to ask her if she was OK – but the next minute I heard a loud thud. I jumped up to find out what was happening but because we'd only just moved in I wasn't familiar with the room and I didn't know where the light switches were. When I found her she wasn't moving, she was just lying deadweight so I panicked. I'd gone mentally and physically because as well as suffering the shock of what was happening to her, I was also feeling the effects of whatever had caused her to collapse. I was worried sick because I didn't know what had caused it, I still couldn't find the light switch and so much was going through my head. I knelt down and went to open her mouth but her jaw had locked and I heard her throat and chest making a croaking sound. When all of that is happening in the pitch dark, you start to fear the worst. I started wondering how I was going to break the news to her family. How would they take it? Was it my fault? Could I have done anything to prevent it?

My legs had turned to jelly but I managed to drag her towards the back door, although I must have looked as if I was drunk as I was doing it, but the house was still new to me, I didn't know my way around it and I couldn't find the key so I staggered downstairs and, by chance, found the front door. I was getting delusional and increasingly more anxious as it went on but I eventually managed to find the key and, after fumbling at the door, I managed to unlock it and drag her outside into the open air, away from whatever was making us ill. I gave her a can of Red Bull and a pair of wellington boots to rest her head on, I don't know why, I think they were just the closest thing at hand. Within 30 seconds she coughed, spluttered and came round. The Red Bull didn't give her wings but it did help her regain consciousness which was a massive relief. We went to hospital and there, after undergoing several tests, we were informed she had suffered from carbon monoxide poisoning.

I could have ended up in the same state as her because I was there too, but because she is small-framed, it affected her more. It seems that how severely you're affected is governed by weight and lung capacity so I was fine because

I was a fatty! They didn't test me in the hospital but I didn't have the same symptoms so that wasn't a problem, it was her I was worried about. We stayed in hospital for 10 hours while she was treated on oxygen and the story made the front page of the Evening Gazette, our local newspaper. I was used to being on the back page but now I'd made it onto page one!

It was a frightening experience. I'd read stories in the past about people who had died from carbon monoxide poisoning. It's such a sad way to go – you go to sleep thinking there's nothing wrong with you, and then you don't wake up. One of the nurses at the hospital told us that if she hadn't stepped out of bed when she did, we'd both have ended up dead because the fumes were still rising up the stairs and into our bedroom from the fireplace downstairs. The silent killer, they call it so there's no doubt we had a very, very lucky escape. In fact the experience disturbed me so much that I slept in my car the following night, I just couldn't bring myself to go to sleep in the house.

Now it seemed pretty obvious that lighting the coal fire had been the cause of our ordeal, and the fact the smoke had been coming out into the living room the way it was suggested there was a blockage in the chimney. I had documentation to say the chimney had been cleared and that all necessary work had been carried out, but it certainly didn't seem like that had been the case. Why else would we have got carbon monoxide poisoning? There were no carbon monoxide detectors in the house either, but we've got one now and I'd urge everyone to get one because you simply never know when you are at risk.

The following day you couldn't move in the house for workmen sent round by the landlord. There were guys cleaning out the chimney, clearing this and clearing that and freeing the windows which were jarred shut. I'd already raised the issue of the windows with the landlord and I asked him what we would do in the case of a fire. Fire has always been a fear because my father lost his sister and her daughter in a fire in Glasgow.

It was suggested I should sue the landlord and I also had a barrister phone me from London asking me what was going on and whether I needed legal assistance. I told him people were round working on the chimney and he told me I shouldn't have let them do that as they were probably putting things right before it could be proved there was a problem with the chimney. But I wasn't after retribution, I was just glad that everyone was OK, including my dogs. We had recovered from the effects of the carbon monoxide and I just wanted to make sure we weren't going to be in the same situation again.

I've since discovered that carbon monoxide poisoning can cause death or brain damage and that we weren't all clear for a six-month period. But there were no casualties, which was the most important thing, and hopefully the landlord has learned his lesson that there must be zero chance of this happening at any of his properties because if she hadn't got out of bed that night, he'd have had two dead tenants on his hands.

MY MATE
PARKY

WHEN I was at Boro, one of my big mates was Gary Parkinson. The players in the team were all good pals but Parky, Mark Proctor and I were particularly close for a few years. Proc and Parky were family men so we didn't socialise away from the club but in the dressing room and on the training pitch we got on very well.

If you had a daughter and you wanted her to marry someone suitable, you'd have picked Parky. He was one of those kids you'd have chosen without hesitation. He was a clean-living Thornaby lad, down to earth, very nice guy, smart – he had everything going for him. Sadly in September 2010 Parky had a stroke and was left with locked-in syndrome, a condition where the patient is fully aware of what's going on but is unable to move or communicate verbally due to complete paralysis of pretty much all their muscles except for their eyes.

But even now whenever you see Parky he's always smartly dressed. He's obviously still in his wheelchair but he doesn't need breathing apparatus any more and we're hoping and praying that in time he'll be able to communicate with his mouth. He gets physio on a regular basis but he needs 24-hour-a-day attention and he has a lift in his house to get between floors. He still likes a bet and Tony Mowbray gave him a scouting role when he was manager of Boro, and he'd watch through the videos of players that were sent to him. Needless to say I had a dig at him when I saw him and told him he'd recommended some right donkeys! We always try to make him laugh when we visit. He likes to watch all sports on the television, so he has plenty to keep himself occupied. He also came to the Riverside on Boxing Day 2013 with his family for Boro's game against Blackpool and it was great to see him there. To start with I think he was cocooned in his own world – he didn't want to communicate with anyone on social media and shied away from public appearances – and I totally understand that - but since then he's been out and about a bit. He played for Preston when David Moyes was the manager, and he went to Old Trafford to watch a game when Moyesie was in charge of Manchester United. Moyesie has been to visit him a good few times and so too has Owen Coyle, his former team-mate at Bolton. Parky is such a decent bloke that he's never been short of visitors.

When I first heard about Parky's condition, I mentioned to one of my mates that someone should do something for him. It was quite clear he was going to need a lot of care and that it was going to take a lot of money and it seemed to me that a fund-raising dinner would be a terrific way to do it. My mate agreed completely but he asked "Why are you trying to put it on to someone else? Why don't you do it?" I slept on it and the following morning my mind was made up – I was going to organise a fund-raising event. I got in touch with every player from the 1986 Boro squad, plus manager Bruce Rioch and coach Colin Todd too, and asked them if they would be interested. I hadn't spoken to some of them since I'd left the club but every one of them, without hesitation, said they were up for it, including Gary Hamilton who was living in America. I was well in with the Tall Trees in Yarm because it was like a second home to me and I'd always been made welcome there, so that was the obvious place to hold it. I spoke to Lal Kawndele, who worked under the owner Javed Majid, and he told me the venue would hold around 800 people, which seemed fine. I publicised it through my own website and in the Evening Gazette, explaining how important the funds were to Gary's family and that all the team would be there, and the interest was fantastic. I phoned Lal to tell him that I had around

700 people coming and we were still months away, but about a week later I had to call him back to say we had more than 800. So it went on, with me phoning Lal with the latest figure and asking him if he could squeeze everyone in. We ended up with 1,100 people crammed in with four or five tables on the stage and more on the elevated areas around the periphery of the hall. We raised £32,000, which all went to Parky, so we were delighted and it says so much about him that it was such a successful evening.

I've been a few times to visit Parky since his stroke and despite his condition, if you say something daft or funny, he'll laugh uncontrollably. Mentally he's still tuned in and he's aware of everything that is going on around him. To start with he communicated by blinking, his wife Deborah would go through the alphabet and he'd blink his eyes at the letter he wanted to spell out the words he wanted to convey. He did this to send me a message on the night of our fund-raising dinner at the Tall Trees, although at one point I thought he was going to say something rude! As he chose the letters to spell out the words, they gradually appeared one by one on the big screen we had on the stage. I was waiting with baited breath when I stared at the unfolding message on the screen which read "Bernie you are a t" because I was convinced he was going to say I was a twat! As it turned out the full message was "Bernie you are a top man."

It was a fantastic night, with everyone digging deep to raise a tidy sum and one of the highlights was the auction of signed memorabilia. Thanks to the help of Boro fan and FA bigwig Adrian Bevington, former Boro player Jaime Moreno had brought over a shirt signed by David Beckham who, like him, was playing in America at the time. Becks is obviously a massive name so that was always going to be one of the most sought-after lots. At the end of the night we were talking to a lad who mentioned he had to go to a cashpoint in Yarm to get enough money to pay for the shirt which he'd won in the auction. Fine, we thought no more of it. But the following morning when we went back down to the hall we discovered there were three items missing – Stewart Downing's boots, tickets for a West End show and the Beckham shirt. The boots were found on the stage because whoever won them hadn't taken them and then the tickets turned up too, but the Beckham shirt was still missing and no-one had paid for it. Surely no-one would nick anything like that from a charity event?

A week or two passed and we were still no closer to finding out what had happened to it – it had disappeared into thin air. Then one day I was in a memorabilia shop near the Real Radio studios which I used to get shirts and suchlike framed for our Three Legends events. While I was in there we were talking about the Parky dinner and I mentioned that someone had taken the Beckham shirt without paying for it. At that, the shop owner's ears pricked up – someone had been on the phone asking if they wanted to buy a signed Beckham shirt just a few days earlier. The guy had left his number so the shop owner phoned him, asked him how much he wanted for it and established it was identical to the one which had gone missing. In fact there was no doubt it had to be the same one. Both myself and Micky Horswill, who had compered the auction on the night were furious – especially when it transpired we knew the identity of guy who had the shirt and that he was a pal of Jon Kirby, who was my boss at the radio station. We got Jon involved and Micky and I made it clear we'd go to the press with the story if his mate didn't bring the shirt back or pay for it. Sure enough he turned up with it half an hour before the deadline we'd set him. He insisted it was all a big mistake and spun us some rich yarn about how he'd bought it from someone in Yarm, but it simply didn't add up to us, especially as the guy in question had been involved in dodgy dealings in the past.

But we didn't let that sour a great night for a great bloke. I've got stacks of great memories of Parky when we played together. He trained hard, he was a good footballer and he always had a smile on his face. He was good for the town because he was one of the local lads who helped Boro out of the liquidation nightmare and then promotion from the Third Division to the First. He wore the shirt with pride, as most of the lads did in those days.

He was a right-back by trade but he was good at going forward and had a great shot - he beat some of the best keepers around.

One time he didn't get a chance to put one away, though, was when we played Ipswich Town in the Premier League. The score was 2-2 going into the last minute of the game when we were awarded a penalty. Parky had been out with injury and I hadn't scored for a while so we were both eager to get on the scoresheet. I picked the ball up but Parky went to grab it off me because he wanted to take the spot kick as well. There was a lot of going to and fro, and arguing over who should take it before I finally got my way. I put the ball down on the spot, took a run-up and crashed it into the Holgate End! The fans were giving me all sorts of stick for it so as we got into the dressing room I went up to Parky and said "I told you that you should have taken it!" He didn't see the funny side at the time but I've brought it up recently and he seems to have forgiven me!

As I've mentioned before, when Lennie Lawrence took over as manager of Boro, he made it plain he was looking for new heroes, so that made me, Proc and Parky the outcasts as we were part of the establishment. It obviously wasn't nice knowing you weren't wanted but we could still laugh about it and many a time Proc or I would stick a note under Parky's hotel room door the night before a game saying "You're getting the axe" or "You're not playing tomorrow".

The first time I went to see him after his stroke it came as quite a shock. As I approached his room in the hospital I could see him, sideways on, in a wheelchair with his head supported and breathing apparatus in. It was one of those situations where you think "What do I say here? What do I do? How do I deal with it?" I decided it would be best to just be me, so I went in, said some daft things and he started laughing which made me realise it was all worth it and that there was a bit of fight in there. I relaxed after that and I've been there a few times since.

The last time my father came down from Glasgow to Middlesbrough to visit me, he insisted that even though he wasn't well himself he should go to see Parky because he knew him too. He was friends with Parky's dad and they used to sit together at Ayresome Park on matchdays. There's a story that on one afternoon a guy over to the right of them was giving Parky stick non-stop throughout the game – so Parky's dad went over and stuck one on him!

It's a long and arduous road but hopefully things will start to look up for Parky. He's certainly in good hands. His family have been terrific. He met his wife, Deborah, when she was still at school and she has been an absolute rock. He's got a wonderful, smart-looking and educated family around him and they are all a credit to him. You can never give up hope, it's just a case of hoping and praying that he makes a recovery. Parky is one of the most genuine lads I've ever met and it's so sad that this sort of thing only ever seems to happen to the good guys while murderers and rapists walk the streets until they are 100.

Recently myself Pally and Proc have visited Gary. He is at home, has 24 hr care, a lift. He loves TV football and a bet on the horses.

The Gary Parkinson Trust Fund has been set up to help Parky's rehabilitation – if you'd like to donate or find out more information, visit www.garyparky.co.uk

Alongside Parky celebrating another victory.

AN ANIMAL
LOVER

I'VE always been a massive animal lover. In a way animals are better than humans because they don't talk back, they don't ask for much and they always seem to be happy. In fact I love animals so much that as of October, 2014 I've been a vegetarian.

I can't bear the thought of animals suffering, especially unnecessarily and I've always been the same. I remember on one of our trips to Singapore, we paid a visit to Indonesia. We were all feeling pretty hungry after the boat ride so we headed off to a floating restaurant where one of the specialities was lobster – and you got to choose your own. I wasn't a vegetarian at the time but I couldn't do it. These creatures of the sea were still alive and I just couldn't pick one to be thrown into a pot of boiling water so I just sat there and ate nothing. There was also a massive turtle living in a glass tank in the restaurant. Whether it was on the menu or not I've no idea but it certainly wasn't in its natural habitat and didn't have a great deal of space to swim about and do whatever turtles do when they're not it captivity. To me, it was just wrong, keeping it like that so I asked Gary Gill, who was also on the trip, if he fancied going halves with me so we could buy this turtle and set it free. Gilly was happy to come in with me for it but the restaurant manager was adamant that it wasn't for sale.

I became a vegetarian after reading about and looking at pictures of animal cruelty, which I'd done many times before I made the conscious decision to stop eating meat. Even before that there were certain things I wouldn't eat – lamb for example – and I remember watching that smarmy bastard Piers Morgan on TV swanning around somewhere exotic talking about the rich and famous and how they enjoyed the so-called delicacy of foie gras, which is a fattened duck or goose liver. I watched video footage later to confirm what I already knew, namely that force-feeding procedures are used by putting a tube down the bird's throat and into its stomach to fatten the livers so if that's not cruel, what is? It really annoys me that if you or I kicked our dog or cat – which I'd never do by the way, I'm just using it as an example – it would be classed as animal cruelty and we'd get arrested. But if a big company does something like this it's OK because they're making money. Double standards? You bet. We should return the compliment by throwing these pompous bastards in a cage and sticking a tube down their throats. I'd happily do it. Fox hunting is another example of where one rule applies to us and another to them. I'd love to tell those posh bastards to get off their horses and run into the countryside. I'd tell them ten minutes later my mates and I would get on the horses, chase them, test their blood-pressure,when we find them and then let the dogs rip them to shreds. Tell us it's not a bloodthirsty sport then.

My musical hero Morrissey, a very vocal vegetarian and never one to shy away from hard-hitting and controversial comments on the subject, caused a storm when he compared fast food chains with the massacre of 76 people in Norway by right-wing extremist Anders Brehring Breivik in 2012. Just before playing Meat Is Murder during a gig in Poland he told the crowd "We all live in a murderous world, as the events in Norway have shown, with 97 dead. Though that is nothing compared to what happens in McDonald's and Kentucky Fried shit every day." He went too far with that, way too far. You can't compare the two, but I can see where he's coming from, because what the big companies get away with is unbelievable.

Living where we do, I often see sheep or pigs cooped up on the back of a wagon and it's obvious there's only one place their journey is going to end and that's in hell, or the slaughterhouse as it's known. It makes me frustrated and sad and I'd love to let the lot of them out, honestly I would. As Sir Paul McCartney once said,

"If slaughterhouses had glass walls, everyone would be a vegetarian." I agree with that. Have a look on the internet and see what they do to pigs, cows and other animals and I guarantee it will shock you because it's really disturbing.

My mate Eric Gates is a pig farmer and he used to invite me up to his farm to see the piglets being born. I used to visit him regularly, as I've mentioned before, and I'd see them get bigger and bigger before, just like that, they would disappear. I'm not knocking Gatesy because that's the business he's in so it's his prerogative and the animals were all free-range, well looked after and well-fed and watered, but despite their luxurious surroundings, the outcome was always the same for most of them

My son, Ryan is vegetarian too – in fact he stopped eating meat long before me and I'd always admired him for that. I'd been playing Meat Is Murder by The Smiths one day and he asked me what it was about so I told him. He was at Stokesley School at the time and not long after our conversation the pupils were shown videos about the meat industry. If he'd been thinking about it before, that made his mind up. We knew something was afoot when his mum asked me if I'd lifted the bacon out of the fridge. Of course I hadn't but the bacon had gone missing not once, but twice. I got Ryan and his brother Dominic together and asked them to explain what was going on because someone had moved it and it wasn't me or their mum! Ryan owned up and admitted he'd hidden it so I told him it was fine if he wanted to become a vegetarian but that it wasn't for him to say what everyone else in the house should or shouldn't eat. So first it was him – although my mother insists she's a vegetarian even though she eats chicken - and then me.

So because of my love for animals, you can see how outraged I'd be if ever I was accused of mistreating one. But that's exactly what happened. During the time my da was ill and I was making trips up to Glasgow to visit him, I had a pony. Every day it was fed and watered and I always made sure its nails were cut – I love animals so there was no way it wasn't going to be well looked after. But one day while I was up visiting my father I had a phone call to say the pony was running loose, and the RSPCA got involved. The next thing I knew, I had the RSPCA on the phone telling me I was being cruel to an animal. You what? I honestly had no idea what they were on about. Even though I was away in Glasgow I made sure someone was going in every day to feed and water my pony so I really couldn't comprehend what the problem was. When all came to all, they reckoned one nail was overgrown. One nail, out of four hooves. I ended up receiving a caution because of it, although when I took it up with one of my mates who is a vet, he told me it was a load of rubbish. OK, that nail may have needed attention and, as the pony's owner, that was down to me. But I had other things on my mind – my father was dying so

I was up and down the motorway visiting him and in any case it was a pretty minor issue and the pony was walking fine. I certainly wasn't starving it or anything like that.

As a result of my apparent "mistreatment" of the pony, I had it taken off me. Yet the guy who had got me to sign the paperwork had the cheek and audacity to ask me if I wanted another pony! You're having a laugh, aren't you? If I was cruel to the one you've just taken off me, why are you asking if I want another one? After I'd been to the World Cup with the Republic of Ireland in 1990, I donated a couple of signed shirts to the RSPCA because I'm a big animal lover, but this was another side of the organisation I hadn't seen before and I wouldn't do anything to raise money for them again.

I had another run-in with them when I tried to get a dog from them. I had money at the time but rather than buy one from a breeder, I thought I'd get a stray from the RSPCA. I knew I could give a good home to a dog that needed one and, as an animal lover, it seemed a good thing to do. So I visited the kennels, chose a wee mongrel, signed the papers and asked if I could take it away. Apparently I couldn't, however, until they had checked over where I lived.

I already had a dog and where I lived the views were outstanding, behind the house was a massive field and the fence around my garden was chest height so, although I'd expected to sign the papers and take the new addition to the family home there and then, I couldn't foresee any problems. It wasn't, however, good enough for the RSPCA. The officer who came to visit had a good look around, then told me the fence wasn't high enough. The dog was knee height, the fence was chest height, I couldn't understand it. "It's a dog I'm getting, not a kangaroo," I said to the guy from the RSPCA but he was adamant I wasn't getting the dog unless I made the fence bigger. It was plenty high enough for my other dog and, even if it did get out, there was a huge field on the other side, so was that really a problem? As a result I never did get the dog and I lost my faith in the RSPCA, which is a shame. I know they do some great work, but my dealings with them have tainted my opinion of them.

I've had animals for years and at the moment I have two young pups, two Irish setters and a cat. And I'm certainly not cruel to them! In fact when I was away with the Republic of Ireland at the World Cup in Italy, I used to talk to my Irish setter on the phone. It's true! Whenever I phoned home to talk to my then wife Karen, I'd ask her to put the dog on. I'd say "Hello Sean (that was his name), good boy, are you alright?" Every morning when we went to breakfast Jack Charlton would say "Have you spoken to your dog, Bernie?" I always used to joke that I talked to the dog because I got more sense out of it than anyone else in the squad, but the truth is that I'm an animal lover and I've always cared about my pets.

My ten-year-old female dog Penny sadly had to be put down in July 2013. I'd been taking her to the vet for months because she had a cough which just didn't seem to clear up, and one night she started to bring up thick, white mucus. I took her to an emergency vet at one o'clock in the morning and was told it was a heart problem. She was restless all that night and I knew I had to make the heart-breaking decision and have her put out of her misery. With previous dogs I'd managed to pass the responsibility to someone else and it was no different this time, and the following morning I picked her up, carried her to the car – because she was unable to walk – before she was taken back to the vet. Hard though it was, I knew it was the right decision and in fact if I'd had the chance when my father was ill I would have done the same thing. Why should you let the things you love struggle like that when you know it's only going to end one way? It's no quality of life fighting against the tide when there is no chance of a recovery, you're only prolonging their agony. Penny was put down as requested and I've always buried my animals after they have left us but I left her in the car for two days before doing it while I came to terms with losing her. I know that wasn't the most hygienic thing to do but it was my way of dealing with it. After she was put down I did the same as after I'd lost my da and went on a five-mile run to clear my head – some people might turn to drink or drugs when they are grieving, but that's what I do. It's my way of dealing with things.

I've had all sorts of animals over the years and at one time I kept peacocks. I had about a dozen of them so when my mate asked if he could have a few, I was happy to oblige. They were beautiful birds but his surroundings were probably more suitable because he lived in a manor house set in acres of land, so I took a few of the birds over. About a week after delivering them I received a call from my mate asking if they could be returned. It turned out he'd had a ding-dong with his neighbour over them and the only solution was to send them back.

Six months later I was in Glasgow to visit my parents and by chance I noticed in the local paper that Teesside-born comedian Roy 'Chubby' Brown was appearing at the SECC. I asked my old schoolmate Jim Mills if he fancied going to see Chubby and he didn't take much persuading because his sense of humour is pretty much the same. I knew Chubby and Millsy was keen to meet him after the show so we waited until the majority of people had left the venue before I approached one of the crew and asked him to tell Chubby I was there. Twenty minutes later we were backstage and the first thing Chubby said to me was "What about those ****ing peacocks! They've been shitting on my car and all over my conservatory!" It turned out Chubby was my mate's neighbour and the reason I had to take the birds back. He carried on ranting and raving about these peacocks and said his neighbour had helpfully suggested putting up a 40-foot high net to prevent them straying on to Chubby's property but still he wasn't appeased. "Correct me if I'm wrong," he went on, "but they're ****ing birds aren't they? And birds can fly so what good would a net do? They'd just fly over it!" All the while my mate Millsy was dumbfounded and had no idea what Chubby was talking about, in fact he admitted afterwards that he thought we were being treated to a private show.

Before I gathered up the peacocks to transport them I had to catch them and that was easier said than done. Despite my love of birds – I'm talking the feathered sort here although I'm a fan of both types – I knew it was going to be a tough job because they are big, they don't like being intimidated and they can give you a nasty peck. So I came up with a master plan. I left bread and seeds in the garage, left several large bird boxes in there and my mate Colin, who is a big, fearless lad, agreed to catch them once they had gone in. I left the garage door open and, sure enough, in went the birds. Colin arrived and I closed the door immediately from the outside so that he could get down to business. As I waited on the other side of the garage door, all I could hear was crash, bang, wallop, screech, squawk until 20 minutes later when I heard my out-of-breath mate shout "Open the ****ing door!"

When I obliged and lifted the garage door it was as if he'd been in a pillow fight, there were feathers everywhere. There were feathers in his hair, on his clothes and in his mouth – he looked like a giant peacock himself. Fortunately all the birds were fine though, even though they seemed to have put up a bit of resistance to being moved to a new home.

Colin is a good pal and I always used to give him the job of looking after my animals and feeding them whenever I went away. On one occasion when I went on holiday to Spain I phoned him to check everything was OK back at the ranch. Happily all the animals were fine but the same couldn't be said for him! For a start he'd got bitten on the back of his hand while he was feeding the pony. Then when he'd got down on all fours to collect eggs from the chicken coop as I'd suggested he should, one of the cockerels started pecking away at his bum! This cockerel was pretty mad to be fair, it was the one Gatsey had left in the studio and it wouldn't have needed a second invitation and pecking a big, fat builder's arse so it didn't surprise me. Then to cap off an eventful day, he returned to feed the dogs. It was raining outside so he left his shoes in the porch and let the dogs out to run freely for a bit and after he'd called them back in and went to put his shoes back on they had vanished. The dog had obviously taken a fancy to them and ran off with them. He eventually found one of them in the field covered in mud but he never did find out where the other one went. I was lazing by the pool in in sunny Spain in the 80 degree heat when he told me so I thought it was hilarious. I was laughing my head off on the other end of the phone but I could tell he hadn't really seen the funny side of it!

Eric Gates pig and piglets support the Boro!

A MUSICIAN INSTEAD OF A FOOTBALLER?

IF I was young again and had the choice, I think I'd become a singer or a musician instead of a professional footballer. I don't play any instruments – although I did pretend to play the bagpipes once – but I love listening to music because it makes me happy and it can motivate me. When I played at Boro the song I listened to in my car as I arrived at Ayresome Park was Desire by U2 because it really got me pumped up ahead of the game.

I like to think I have a wide taste in music. Prince is the best performer I've ever seen, I love the Rolling Stones and I listen to David Bowie and AC/DC too. But my absolute favourite is Morrissey, I'll listen to something by him every day without fail. I admire him and I'm fascinated by him. I've never met the great man but I'm getting closer and I'm always interested to talk to people who have met him and who know him because I want to find out as much as I can about him. Simple Minds played a gig in Newcastle a few years ago and I managed to meet Jim Kerr, their lead singer, and we started off talking about Celtic because I know he's a big fan and then I switched the conversation to Morrissey. "Come on Jim," I said, "you must have met him." He hadn't, as it happened, but his ex-wife Chrissie Hynde had, and his kids knew him – although in as many words he said they thought he was very strange!

I spoke to Janick Gers, the Iron Maiden guitarist from Teesside, who also said he hadn't met him but he too had heard reports he was a bit on the strange side. Then last year I was down in London for a show on BT Sport hosted by Danny Baker and Danny Kelly. It turned out that Danny Kelly had done loads of interviews with Morrissey when he worked on the NME – so what was he like? Danny told me that back then he was OK but these days he lives in America and could be a bit aloof.

The biggest insight I've had so far is from meeting Cornelius Carr, the boxer, who appears on the video for Morrissey's single Boxers. I'd interviewed Cornelius years ago for Boro TV because he's a Teesside lad but I wasn't aware of the Morrissey connection then. So, having discovered the link, I couldn't wait to find out all about it when I met up with him again. It transpired Morrissey, who is a big boxing fan, was watching one of his fights – for the British super-middleweight belt no less. And as the victorious Cornelius was displaying the belt to his fans after the bout, one of Morrissey's flunkies came over to him and declared "Morrissey would like to see you in the dressing room." Cornelius was in no rush to go back because he was drinking in the atmosphere and celebrating his victory. Cornelius told the guy Morrissey could come up and see him if he wanted to talk to him because he was busy celebrating, and there was a big group of fans who had travelled from Teesside to support him. Morrissey was the last person on his mind, but suddenly he appeared at the ringside to speak to him. He congratulated the new champ on his victory and they had their picture taken together at the ringside, before Morrissey asked him if he'd like to appear on the video. Although Cornelius didn't really know who he was, he agreed. His agent contacted him in due course and he starred in the video for the song – it's on YouTube if you fancy watching it.

Cornelius went on to add that when Morrissey went on tour next, the backdrop was a massive picture of his face. "His mates were saying 'he fancies you'," Cornelius told me when I spoke to him on that second occasion. The pair didn't meet again but when Morrissey was asked about his love of the sport on Jools Holland's TV show, the answer he gave when asked who his favourite fighter was – you've guessed it! Cornelius Carr.

I asked Cornelius if he was a Morrissey fan and he admitted he wasn't, but said that as he'd got older he'd started listening to some of his CDs. He said that although Morrissey comes across as a bit of a sad case, once you listen to his music you get past that – he's really interesting and by listening to his music you get to know how he thinks. The press would have it that he's a pretty complex character – dour, strange and weird even – but Cornelius said he found him to be just a normal guy and not up himself at all. He received a handwritten letter from Morrissey and said he had a strange style of writing, quite childlike in fact. I'd have loved to have seen it myself but unfortunately Cornelius said he didn't have it any more, which is a shame.

I'm intrigued with Morrissey and I've seen him about 14 times in concert. I never saw him with The Smiths because when he was in the band I'd not long moved to Middlesbrough and I was homesick so going back to Glasgow was more important than going to see anyone in concert at the time. I'd got into The Smiths when I worked for the council in Glasgow, cleaning graffiti off walls and tidying gardens. I was about 18 or 19 and there was one guy on the team who stood out like a sore thumb. His hair was dyed jet black and his quiff must have been three feet high! He was always dressed in black and wore eye make-up. He looked a bit of a weirdo to be honest but he fascinated me. One day he was singing this song that went "Let me get my hands on your mammary glands, let me get your head on the conjugal bed." I asked him what it was all about and he told me it was by The Smiths. I'd never heard of them but I gave them a listen and I loved them.

I've seen Morrissey live all over the place. The best one was in Paris. The idea was that I'd spend a couple of days out in the city sightseeing and take in the concert while I was there. The venue was called Le Zenith and as I approached it I thought it was a bit too quiet – there were no weirdos anywhere to be seen! I thought the crowd must already be inside the venue but when I got to the entrance I saw there was a notice up, in French obviously, saying he'd cancelled the gig, Instead of getting annoyed I thought "How cool is that?" He's notorious for not turning up and he'd done it again. He rescheduled it though and I decided to go back out there for it. Rather than spend money on hotels, though, I thought I'd get a Eurostar ticket, spend the day in Paris, see the gig, then get the first Eurostar back to London at six o'clock the following morning. Mozza in Paris, I couldn't miss it. It was a great gig and afterwards I headed back to the station. There were a few drunks, druggies and hippies about but nothing to worry about so I tried to nestle down on a seat to grab a few hours' sleep. I was just getting comfortable when in came the gendarmes with big, vicious dogs and ordered everyone out of the station. It was the middle of November, freezing cold and I had no hotel to go to. So I ended up walking the streets looking for somewhere to bed down again and I ended up sleeping in a doorway. I probably had a couple of hours' sleep before I got up and went for a walk to try and get warm because it was so cold. When I got back to London I had to get straight in the car and drive back up north. As I headed home I thought "I love Morrissey – but not enough to do this again!"

I've met the Pope, I'd love to have met Nelson Mandela and I'd love to meet Morrissey. I wouldn't want to have a big conversation with him, I'd just like to spend some time in his company and have a chat with him. If I could ask him one question it would be, "If there's one person in the world you could shoot, who would it be?" I'm sure he'd appreciate that question. I wouldn't want to shoot anyone myself and I'd have sooner gone to jail for being a conscientious objector than join the Army in wartime, but I'm sure Morrissey would have someone in mind! If she was still alive, it may well have been Margaret Thatcher. He was a fierce critic of the former Prime Minister and he once remarked that whoever murdered her he would marry, male or female! I like him because he's opinionated and he doesn't care who he upsets, he says what he wants. I like his music and I like his lyrics but I also admire his attitude. I'm genuinely not sure if I'd like his company but I like what he's about. Footballers don't intrigue me in the way that Morrissey does and even though Lionel Messi is a great player, for instance, he's not a character. He's faceless. You can't say that about Morrissey.

He was asked in one interview about his performances and he replied "I don't perform, only seals perform." He's always coming out with some great quotes and one of my favourite was his answer after being asked if The Smiths would ever reform. He said "I'd rather eat my own testicles – and that's saying something coming from a vegetarian." Because he loves to be controversial and to rub people up the wrong way, he's always going to leave himself open to criticism and judgement from others but he's never short of a reply. When Richard Madeley had a pop at him on one occasion, calling him "an insufferable puffed-up prat," and a "vainglorious strutting humbug" his comeback was "I think that's a bit rich coming from a man who actually married his mother."

There's a story that an American manager, who looked after probably the biggest solo artist in the world, wanted to meet Morrissey and flew over from Los Angeles to the studio where he was working. Morrissey walked into the studio behind him but then disappeared and couldn't be found anywhere. Eventually the guy just left and when Morrissey reappeared, his reason for going off was simple "I didn't like his hair." What a character! Mind you I've disappeared from presentations and also when I was meant to get circumcised!

On the 21st March 2015, I travelled to see the Morrissey gig in the state of art Hydro in my home city Glasgow. His interval film show was full of his personal touches. Starting off with The New York Dolls and finishing off with the words Margaret Thatcher Is Dead LOL., to which 'Ding Dong the Witch Is Dead' was played. As he took the stage his opening song was The Queen is Dead with a backdrop that had the Queen giving a one fingered salute, this changed to William and Kate and the words United King-dumb.He mentioned his disappointment at Scotland not voting yes in the referendum. I have wittnessed him perform Meat Is Murder before, but this time it was more visually distrubing and he changed the lyrics to "Lamb, ham bacon, spam its murder, but do you care? Do you care? Do you care?"

Morrissey plays at the Town Hall Middlesbrough.

Morrissey playing in the City of Culture (Glasgow).

Morrissey and Cornellius Carr the boxer from Middlesbrough.

In bed with Moz!

With Jim Kerr lead singer of Simple Minds in Newcastle.

aximo Park front man Paul Smith at the Holgate wall Middlesbrough.

BACK AT
THE BORO

PERSONALLY I feel I was overlooked by Middlesbrough for too long with regards to hosting guests on a matchday at the Riverside Stadium. Club legends such as Jim Platt, Alan Peacock, Gordon Jones and Stuart Boam were all rightly brought in to start the whole thing off. It's a great opportunity for fans to not only watch the match and have a good meal but also to spend some time in pleasant surroundings with one of the big names who has been there and done it with the club, and they were all guys who fit the bill perfectly. They played hundreds of games, they were loyal and loved by the supporters. But as the years progressed some left their roles and other former players were brought in to replace them as matchday hosts in one of the rooms at the stadium – people who played a quarter of the games I did for the club and scored nowhere near the number of goals. OK, so I was working on the radio on a matchday for a large chunk of that time, but so was Craig Hignett and it wasn't a problem for him, and Neil Maddison does it now so they've obviously working around broadcasting duties doesn't present a problem. Why couldn't they have gone for me?

I always knew that, given the opportunity, I could do a good job as a matchday host. All the time I was being overlooked I'd think "What could I bring to the room?" Well I could bring fun, opinions and knowledge. I'm sure a lot of the players they've had doing the job had the knowledge, but opinions and a bit of fun about them? I don't think so. A lot of them were a bit straight-laced.

But last summer Neil Maddison, who I do a bit of coaching with, told me that the club wanted to talk to me about being a match-day host. What me? Surely not! I thought it was a joke. I'd been overlooked for years, I can only surmise because of my opinions, so I was convinced this apparent U-turn was some kind of wind-up. A few weeks went by and I didn't hear anything but then, sure enough, the club contacted me and asked if I'd go in and see them for chat. I still couldn't imagine they wanted to offer me a matchday host role and I started thinking "Surely they don't want me to play – I'm 53 and far too old to make a comeback! My back's gone and so have my knees!" But when I arrived and the meeting got underway, they said that they would love me to host the Legends Lounge, which is the biggest hospitality area in the stadium. I was waiting for them to add that I couldn't say this and I couldn't do that and I had a reply all ready. But they didn't say that. Instead they told me they wanted me just to be myself and that sold it for me. I'm not going to be dominated or dictated to, I'll always be exactly who I am, so I was happy to accept the offer.

I went into it knowing that it was important not to overdo it because it's their club and I respect that – I'm not daft – but if I have an opinion, I'll give it freely. If the team played crap, I'm not going to tell people they were good! If you don't say what you truly believe, then you're conning the public. Some people are so sycophantic and up the club's backside that they believe you're not a fan if you say something against the team. What a load of absolute rubbish! If I make a comment about something it's because I want to see change and improvement. If you've got a family you'll love your kids more than anything, but you'll criticise them because you want to make them better and put them on the right track. It's because you care not because you want to ruffle feathers or unsettle people. Football is no different. If I can criticise my sons, I can criticise millionaires! I criticised myself when I played too. If I'd scored a hat-trick I wouldn't dwell on those three goals, I'd be thinking about the ones I missed. I'd be running it through my mind and thinking what I could do to try and make sure the ball went in next time. Bruce Rioch seemed to be on my back all the time, but he was doing it for my own good. I didn't enjoy it, I didn't want to hear it and I wanted to respond, but it was done for a reason and when I look back I can see how good he was for me.

After that initial meeting, the club put out a press release saying "Bernie's back" although in truth I've never been away. I've always been at the Riverside for Boro's home games, the only difference is that I'm working for the club now. They measured me for suit although it wasn't ready for when we had a photoshoot to get some pictures for the website and to publicise my new job. I thought it would be a good idea to try on Jim Platt's suit for size but I soon realised that some temporary adjustments were going to be needed if I was going to wear it for the cameras. Jim is a lot bigger than me and when I put his jacket on, it was like a coat! And his trousers – I'm sure they'd been made for Chubby Brown!

I like the contact with football supporters, so it's a great job to have. We've done talk-ins throughout the North-East over the years with the Legends and we've had some great laughs so being in the company of Boro fans every matchday is right up my street. It's a different clientele in the Legends Lounge - I'm mixing with the prawn sandwich brigade! But I'll tell you what, they're the roughest prawn sandwich brigade you'll ever meet. They're a fantastic bunch of people, though, and I'd far sooner mix with them than a bunch of pompous twats.

I bring along a special guest to each match and my old mate Gary Pallister filled that role when I hosted my first match against Birmingham in August last year and since then I've had Gordon McQueen, Malcolm Macdonald, Stuart Ripley, Adrian Bevington – the managing director of Club England, Roy Chubby Brown the comedian– and Middlesbrough's international long jump star Chris Tomlinson along with me, to name but a few. When Rippers came along he told a story from our days together in the Boro team that I'd forgotten about. I mentioned in an earlier chapter how footballers enjoy a bit of hi-jinks, and Rippers gave the Legends Lounge his own insight into football humour when he told them about the time we were staying in a hotel for an away game and he discovered, as he was getting dressed, that Archie Stephens had done a poo in his sock! He didn't know it was Archie at the time of course, but he was in no doubt what was in his sock.

After the game I tell the fans that if they want to have a go at the team or at me, then go ahead. There are always around 150-200 people in the room and after one match this lad stood up to say something so I handed him the microphone. He looked at me and said "Do you know what? I don't like you!" He's not the only one to feel like that to be fair, so I told him that was fine. It didn't bother me. "No, I'm serious," he went on, "I've never liked you."

He seemed really keen to make the point, but I just told him "It's OK, I get your drift." I'd asked if anyone wanted to have their say and told them to be honest, so I suppose I couldn't complain.

Some people are there every week, others you only see once or twice. One week in came a guy dressed up as Chubby Brown, the comedian. There he was, sat in a multi-coloured jacket and trousers with a flying helmet on his head, looking just like Chubby so I asked him if he was funny and, with a completely straight face, he replied "No". He was right as well.

I'd been a guest in lounges throughout the stadium many times so I knew what it was all about. I was pleasantly surprised to be asked to do the job but I couldn't help wondering why the sudden change? I've always been here and the club know what I've achieved but, anyway, they asked me, I accepted and I'm delighted to be involved. Amazingly in the same week I was asked to appear on the BBC. Over the years the Beeb have always shunned me but I was invited onto John Foster's radio show and, again, I was happy to do it.

Maybe a few doors are opening now after the door on the Legends closed. Money has never been my god and I just want to do things that I enjoy and be happy and I'm fortunate that I'm doing that. From my point of view I'd love this to be a long term commitment, although it depends on the club. If I'm sacked as quickly as some of the others guys who have done the job before me, I'd probably never go back to the Riverside. One guy only lasted a week! At least I've managed to get further than that.

I'm also enjoying hosting the Bernie Does Boro phone-in after every match on Community Voice FM. It's a rough and ready phone-in with me saying to fans, "Come on, give me a call and tell it to me like it is". Nothing is vetted – unlike the BBC – and whether you're harshly critical or blowing smoke up the club's arse, I don't care. I just want to hear your opinions. Give me stick or agree with me, I'm easy either way. There's no muzzle on the fans, they're free to talk about what they want, as long as they don't swear.

So now I'm back at the Boro, could I end up doing Boro commentaries again? Who knows? I was on the BBC last year for the first time since 1986 and that was a turn-up for the books. I've played in charity games with other former pros and the BBC have spoken to them for some comments to be broadcast but not me. I'm convinced that if the BBC had commercial radio stations, they'd want me on doing commentaries. I'm experienced and I've got big opinions but unlike the commercial stations who need to keep bringing in the listeners to satisfy the people putting the money in, the BBC don't need a big fan base. They don't need to hit figures because we're paying for it so they can just bob along with no pressure on them, and that's unfair. Would I like to do commentaries again? Of course I would. Could I do it? Of course I could. And if they wanted the best, they'd pair me with Ali Brownlee again because we were the best, the figures proved that. They've never recreated what we had since. Over the years Paul Kerr has worked with Ali, Gary Gill went in after him, then came Craig Hignett and now Neil Maddison is doing the job. Only Paul Kerr didn't have a post with the club, so you can see a pattern emerging there.

Since Ali went to the BBC we've spoken maybe five or six times. We were involved in the book business and a few things went wrong so we had a few verbal ding-dongs and then when he had a surprise 50th birthday party, whoever organised it didn't invite me. I sent him a text that night saying "Have a great night, sorry I didn't get an invite". To me, if you're my mate you're my mate whoever you work for, but Ali seemed to put a bit of distance between us when he went to the BBC, as if I was a bit wild for his company now. I don't know that for sure, I'm only surmising, but that's the way it seems. We used to go to the Tall Trees together every Thursday, but when he joined the BBC he started going to the Thistle in Middlesbrough with Gilly instead.

Another incident that left a sour taste in my mouth came after we'd lost the commentary deal but were still allowed to do 30-second flashes from each game, which Ali did. Century still had the rights to commentate on Newcastle United games so when they were at the Riverside for the Boro match my gaffer, Jon Kirby, told me he wanted me to be the summariser with Bob Moncur, the former Newcastle player, doing it from a Toon perspective. But after I'd arrived at the ground John Simons, one of the group managers, came in with Ali behind him and said he didn't want me to be the summariser, he wanted Ali to do it. Bob was doing it from the Newcastle angle so surely the Boro man had to be an ex-player as well? Otherwise it would be like me taking over the commentary, it just wouldn't work. But apparently

having a commentator as a summariser was perfectly OK, for some obscure, outrageous reason. I was furious and instead of sharing a car with Ali up to the studio Newcastle like we usually did for our show on the Sunday, I made my own way there and told him exactly what I thought when I saw him. I know what I would have done if I was him, I'd have told the ex-player that was a job for him and not me. I'd had to take a back seat while Ali was getting paid to do flashes all season and this was my one chance to get a couple of quid but he took a footballer's job. Ali's a charitable guy and he's helped me a lot but on that occasion he let me down. But that said, we were the best and we could do the job again, given the chance.

The club has totally transformed over the last few years. They listen to the fans, they work in tandem with Twe12th Man who are allowed to chant and bang the drum, to generate a great atmosphere at the Riverside.

The club has meetings with the fans and no one is isolated.Steve Gibson is doing what he does best, backing the current manager and keeping out of the limelight. Long may it continue.

Chubby Brown came in the Legends Legends Lounge as my guest and I wasn't sacked

Promotion shot for my Riverside return.

MY

FAMILY

I'VE very few regrets in life but the biggest one is messing up the family who loved me – the family who backed me, supported me and cared for me. When I look back I can see it was a selfish decision and, because I have a conscience, it still bites away at me every day. Karen, my ex-wife, came to Middlesbrough from Glasgow to support me in my profession. We had a family but I walked out and let them all down emotionally, mentally and physically, and that continues to be a burden I carry. The saying goes that it's easier to leave than be left behind but I've never experienced that. There's another saying that you make your bed and lie in it, and that you get what you deserve. Maybe that's why I've suffered divorce, depression and bankruptcy and I can accept that. I'm a firm believer that you do get what you deserve if you do people wrong. I can only imagine what my family has had to go through and the trauma it has caused them.

Middlesbrough is a goldfish bowl so every sighting, rumour or story was reported back to Karen, which must have been horrendous for her and our two boys, Ryan and Dominic. It's bad enough for Joe Bloggs – and I don't mean that disrespectfully – but with me being on the radio two hours a night, having a column in the Gazette and with the profile I have on Teesside, everyone wanted to badmouth me, tell stories or dish the dirt. It's funny because none of my mates would mention anything even though they knew what was going on, but Karen's so-called friends wanted to tell stories, a lot of them inaccurate.

The bottom line is that I committed adultery. But unlike in a lot of failed marriages, I am still welcome to go round to the family home in Acklam, where the boys still live with their mother. I still feel a sense of resentment from Karen and Dominic, which is understandable, but I'm really grateful the door is still open. Despite my own financial problems I agreed not to contest anything in the divorce settlement as I was the guilty party, and to this day I have never received a penny of my pension.

And I have to say that, proud as I am of my achievements on the football pitch and on the radio, I'm also enormously proud of my two boys. They're both great lads. My own da was the best father I could have wished for and he's always been the example I've looked up to as I've been bringing my boys up. I'm teetotal because my father used to tell me "If it was any good, I'd do it as well," and that's what I've always told Ryan and Dominic. I'm pleased to say they've taken it on board as well. My father's brother was an alcoholic and lost everything. My da saw what he'd been through and I think that's why he didn't want me to drink. I can see his point completely and although I want them to enjoy themselves, I don't want my boys developing a habit like that which is hard to kick.

A few years ago I decided to do something to raise money and awareness of diabetes, a condition which affects my youngest, Ryan. We hit upon the idea of running a half-marathon together but the question was where? The Middlesbrough Half-Marathon takes place every year but Ryan wasn't keen on doing it so close to home because my profile on Teesside means there would be people coming up to me all day wanting to chat which would have made it more difficult to get on with doing what we were there to do. We considered the Great North Run but that starts in Newcastle and we'd probably end up being chased by Geordies! So someone suggested we go abroad to do it and we decided on the New York Half-Marathon. Good job I was over my fear of flying! I contacted James Cook Hospital in Middlesbrough who put me in touch with someone in New York and I managed to secure two places. We were in! We started training, only to have a spanner thrown in the works when we discovered you had to be 18 or over to enter and Ryan was only 16 at the time. Fortunately I managed to get someone to take his place – a guy called Jonathan Way - and my father said he would pay for my flight.

The run was around Central Park, a distance of about seven miles, through Times Square, along the riverside and then to the finish line – and it started at 7.30 in the morning! When you line up at the start, you take your place according to your race number, and mine was far higher than my mate's so I was up near the front with the Kenyans and the real athletes. They were all doing their stretching exercises and lifting their feet up past their head while I could barely lift my knee. They all had the proper running gear on while I was there in a football shirt and sports shorts – it's fair to say I felt more than a little out of place. And once the race started, they were away and I never saw them again! They would have been able to enjoy the sights – all I saw was pavements and bums. I actually ran the half-marathon in a Newcastle United shirt, by the way, as I agreed to wear the colours of whichever fans of the North-east's big three donated the most to the cause. At last Newcastle had finally won something!

Ryan has type one diabetes. By and large he'll go about his daily life without a problem, but if you don't keep on top of the condition, it can be fatal. The original idea of running the half-marathon was to get Ryan to do it and show other kids with the same condition what they could achieve. If he could do it, so could they. We raised £4,000 from doing it, which was a decent sum, although Ryan was obviously disappointed he couldn't take part. He's old enough now, though, so hopefully the two of us can do the run together some time in the future.

I think it's important to spread the message of how much you can still do with diabetes. Gary Mabbutt played for Tottenham and England, Joe Frazier was world heavyweight boxing champion and beat Muhammad Ali, Halle Berry is a Hollywood superstar, Steve Redgrave won five Olympic rowing gold medals, Neil Young has been a rock star for donkey's years – and they all have diabetes. It's been no barrier to Ryan, either. He's at Middlesbrough Art College now and he's doing well. Hopefully that will continue and, after he's finished his course, he'll go to university. He started to play guitar recently and his fingers began to harden, which is a good thing for a guitarist, but he has to prick his finger every day because of his condition and he was worried he'd have to stop playing. That's when I pointed out that Neil Young is type one too and he's nearly 70 and still playing, and that really perked him up. Goals, aspirations and dreams are there to be followed and aimed for, and it's no different for Ryan.

Ryan being a diabetic hasn't been without its dramas though.

Some years ago we went on a short break to Italy and because he has to inject himself with insulin regularly we had to make sure we took all the daytime pens and night-time pens. We were staying in Sorrento in the Bay of Naples and one day we decided to go on a day trip to Rome. The Colosseum, the Trevi Fountain, St Mark's Square – I'd been there before and it's fantastic so I wanted my boy to see all the sights too. We jumped on a train to Naples and then caught a connecting train to Rome. We had a fantastic day sight-seeing, so good in fact that instead of heading back to Sorrento as we'd planned, we booked into a hotel overnight because we missed the last train back as we were too busy doing and seeing everything we wanted to. We continued to walk the streets of Rome, taking in the sights, but at around nine o'clock that night, Ryan realised he had his insulin with him but not his night-time pen to inject himself. He hadn't long been diagnosed with diabetes and my head was in a spin – this was all new to me and I didn't know what we were supposed to do. I didn't want him nestling down to sleep in our hotel room because I was worried about the consequences, so I told him we'd carry on walking and go around the outskirts of the city.

While we were walking it occurred to me that it might not be a bad idea to visit the local hospital to see if we could get a pen there, so that's where we went. At reception we spoke to an American lady who took us to where we needed to go and when we arrived, I swear it was like a scene out of a movie. There were two ladies there, one had a mass of sticky-up hair like Don King and the other was an old lady with a massive book. The American was trying to translate as they spoke to us in broken English. We needed to know the name of the night-time pen but, because he'd not been using it for long, neither of us could remember it so I had to phone his mother in England. By that time it was one o'clock in the morning and she wondered what on earth was going on but I managed to convince her everything was OK and she gave me the name of the pen. Now if this had happened over here, I'd expect to be given a pen by the hospital and that would be it, problem sorted. But that isn't the way they work over there and instead I was handed a prescription which I had to take to a pharmacy. How were we supposed to get there? And where was it?

By now it was two o'clock and because we were on the outskirts of the city, there wasn't a taxi to be seen anywhere. We walked for about two miles when Ryan had what they call a hypo, where your blood-sugar levels drop, you feel faint, dizzy and start to tremble. I found a bench and I sat him down while I ran back to a security guard we'd passed in a nearby building. I asked him if he had a drink or a biscuit I could take to Ryan – I was trying to explain what was going on and that I needed something to get my son's blood-sugar levels right again but I must have looked like a mad man, especially with the language barrier. I think I managed to get the message across though and he gave me a sachet of sugar which I gratefully accepted and ran back to Ryan with it. As soon as the sugar touched his tongue it perked him up, so off we set again to the chemist. When we got there I rang the bell and a lady who worked there came to the door, but when I produced the prescription she said she couldn't give me the pen. I tried to get her to tell me why but I never did discover the reason. We left empty-handed and the only thing for it was to keep on walking until we found another chemist, which we eventually managed to do at about four o'clock. Surely we'd have better luck here…. Wrong! We only needed one pen, obviously, but the guy here reckoned we'd have to buy a pack of ten which would have set us back something like £300! No chance, pal. By then, though, it was morning which meant Ryan could use his day-time pen so we were out of danger and left the chemist empty-handed. It was pretty scary at times but on the plus side there was nobody about at the Trevi Fountain at five in the morning so we took pictures and stood on the Spanish Steps without being bothered by the millions of other tourists who are normally there too when you visit.

Ryan's biggest fitness problem has been his cartilage. He's played for Marton FC for years and was really frustrated at being out injured. He was advised not to play again initially but he went privately to the Spire Hospital in Newcastle because it was still painful after his operation although he came away from there none the wiser. Then a letter from James Cook Hospital in Middlesbrough dropped on the doormat and it advised him to have the cartilage taken out. I had mine taken out when I was 29 and I can still kick a ball so I told him to go for it. If he doesn't play again then so be it, but I want him to keep training because of his diabetes. If he stays fit it will keep his levels right. He's since heard, too, that the cartilage could be replaced at a hospital in Coventry, so that's something which could yet happen.

His older brother, Dominic, however, doesn't play football any more. He scored a hat-trick one week but soon afterwards he told me he wanted to stop playing. I think it was because other lads' parents were shouting out things like "Your dad would have scored that". Stuff like that doesn't serve any purpose. I'm all for parents encouraging their kids on the pitch, but they should watch what they say. The players on the pitch aren't Messi, Rooney or Ronaldo – they're only kids. They're young and still learning but some of the things I've heard shouted from the touchline are criminal.

Although Dominic doesn't play football, he loves the game and

I'm sure he could tell me the name of every player in the world and he's a massive Boro fan although he doesn't go to matches. Both the lads are England fans, which is fair enough since they're English, and a few years ago I bought them each an England shirt when the World Cup was on. They were glued to the TV every time England were playing and they did it with my blessing – but I did take issue at Dominic turning the volume up for God Save The Queen before the match! I didn't mind them wearing the shirts and watching the game, but that was a step too far! I suppose it goes back to when I was a kid and the TV channels closed down at midnight – the younger generation won't believe that used to happen – and God Save The Queen came on before the screen went blank and a little white dot appeared in the middle. My father used to sprint to the telly and turn it off, muttering something like "We're not listening to that shite!"

I remember picking up Dominic just after he was born and it was like lifting the World Cup, or how I imagine lifting the World Cup would be anyway. He was so delicate and precious. He was my first child and it was frightening really. My other abiding memory of that day was bringing him home. I drew the car up outside the hospital and as I waited for Karen and Dominic to come out, a young foreign lady came up to me and asked for a lift. The rain was absolutely belting down, there were no taxis about and she was obviously in a foreign country so I felt a wee bit sorry for her and agreed. I asked her where she lived and she told me it was over Marton way but as we drew closer she started to get a bit mixed up and wasn't really sure if we should be going left or right. It was a surreal experience. You don't have a baby every day and there I was in the car with a total stranger who couldn't remember where she lived. My little baby is 6ft 4ins with a beard now and he's a laid-back character although I've told him he still needs to keep fit because you might look fit on the outside but you have to be fit on the inside too.

Dominic seems to find it difficult to understand how I'm such a big deal among Boro fans – and that isn't meant to sound big-headed – but I think that's because I'm not a role model as his father. I let him down because I left the family home when I split up with his mother. I have to be honest and admit that if my father had left the family home when I was a kid I'd have been gutted, so I understand why he feels that way.

No matter what I do for my boys, I can't hide from the fact that I let them down and I can't change that. There are billions of people in the world in the same situation but it still has a wee stigma attached to it

The boys still live in Acklam in the family home, which I left, but wherever I am I'll still love them, support them and do my best for them. Ryan was a baby when I left home, and Dominic was two. When they were younger Ryan used to come to the door and beg me not to leave when it was time for me to go and I had phone calls at four o'clock in the morning asking me to come back because he didn't feel well, and I'd always go. It was hard, I can tell you. I was the bad guy for going and wrecking everything for them but there's a lot of stuff they don't know.

I've got out of the financial problems I explained in an earlier chapter but I haven't got money to throw around. In recent years I've lived in rented accommodation, I don't have a house phone, Sky TV or the internet. I like to dress well but the majority of my designer gear, be it shirts, suits or T-shirts are from charity shops. I'm not ashamed to admit that. I'd say I go to charity shops once every couple of weeks and I've picked up some top Armani and Hugo Boss suits doing that. OK they cost £70-80 which is a lot of money for a charity shop, but if you'd bought the same suit in anywhere else it would set you back about £500. Dealing with the homeless over the years has opened my eyes and I'm very grateful for the luxuries I have. Money has never been my god.

My faith is still intact, I remain charitable and I continue to have strong opinions and beliefs, and I'm still the same guy who was brought up on that council estate in Glasgow. At the end of the day we are all equal. We come into this world with nothing and we go out with nothing. The last three decades have certainly been a rollercoaster, as you can see, but I've enjoyed the highs, survived the lows and I'm grateful for what I've got.

Here's to the next 30 years.

True love my newly born son Dominic.

Dossing on the steps in Rome while on holiday with son Ryan.

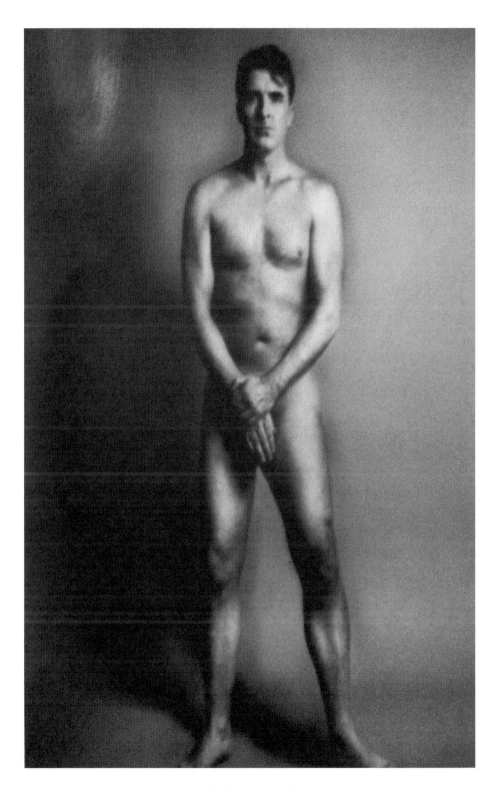

Stripped naked.

Sporting Memories Foundation

Reading this book is sure to have triggered many fond memories of playing or watching football. The Sporting Memories Foundation uses memories of football and sport to bring older sports fans together at grounds, clubs and in community settings across the UK. The groups are provided free of charge and are open to anyone over the age of 50. The friendly, fun activities are designed in particular to support older sports fans who are lonely, living with depression or facing memory problems or dementia.

I'm a supporter of the Sporting Memories Network and proud to be a

patron of the foundation. I have added some of my memories of playing the beautiful game to their website. I hope you enjoy reading them and take time to add some of your own all time favourite moments too. These can then be used in the groups to help trigger yet more conversation and debate! If you can also spare a couple of quid and donate to them even better.

You can find out more about the work and the charity at www.sportingmemoriesnetwork.com

Bernie Slaven is a patron of The Sporting Memories Foundation